Scattered Chapters

Envisioned by Gordon Giltrap (MBE)

Author: Nick Hooper

Inspired by the music of Gordon Giltrap and Paul Ward

Scattered Chapters

Envisioned by Gordon Giltrap (MBE)

Author: Nick Hooper

Inspired by the music of Gordon Giltrap and Paul Ward

WYMER PUBLISHING
Bedford, England

First published in Great Britain in 2022
by Wymer Publishing
www.wymerpublishing.co.uk
Tel: 01234 326691
Wymer Publishing is a trading name of Wymer (UK) Ltd

Copyright © Nick Hooper / Wymer Publishing.

ISBN: 978-1-912782-17-2

The Author hereby asserts his rights to be identified
as the author of this work in accordance with sections
77 to 78 of the Copyright, Designs & Patents Act 1988.

All rights reserved. No part of this publication may be
reproduced or transmitted in any form or by any means,
electronic or mechanical, including photocopying, or any
information storage and retrieval system, without written
permission from the publisher.

This publication is sold subject to the condition that it shall not,
by way of trade or otherwise, be lent, re-sold, hired out or
otherwise circulated without the publishers prior consent in any
form of binding or cover other than that in which it is published
and without a similar condition including this condition
being imposed on the subsequent purchaser.

Every effort has been made to trace the copyright holders of the
photographs in this book but some were unreachable. We would
be grateful if the photographers concerned would contact us.

Design by Andy Bishop / 1016 Sarpsborg
Printed by Harrier LLC.

A catalogue record for this book is available from the British Library.

Contents

Intro	7
Starfield	9
Scattered Chapters	13
Nordkapp	17
One for Billie	19
Sharing Days	23
A Cottingley Secret	27
Through Braden's Door	29
The Constant Friend	33
The Kissing Gate	37
Requiem	43
She Who Gently Smiles	47
The Work of Angels	55
The Stars Look Down on Linda	61
The Wounded Healer	69
Turning Earth	73
Precious	77
The Melody Weaver's Son	79
Heartsong	97
Artist's profile	100

Est. 1993

All The Paintings and Art work in this book were curated by Artifex Gallery some of which are for sale at the gallery and from the website.

I have known Gordon for many years and when asked if I could source different Artists to illustrate the Music and stories in this book, I jumped at the chance to be involved in this project, bringing together 3 different Art forms. It's been amazing to see how each artist has interpreted the music and story in their own styles. I hope it brings a new dimension to the Music and Stories.

Nigel Bates
Director Artifex Gallery

Established in 1992, Artifex Gallery sell the very best in Contemporary British Art & Craft. The 3000sq ft Gallery is housed in a converted farm building at the Mitchell Centre for Art & Craft in Sutton Coldfield.

We specialise in designer/maker furniture and we have a specific gallery room with a selection of one-off pieces of contemporary furniture made by Britain's leading craftsmen. Visitors can buy from the large selection on display or seek inspiration from the maker portfolios and commission their own piece of furniture.

The large first floor of the Gallery is devoted to paintings, all original, featuring the work of a wide variety of artists. We also have extensive displays of ceramics, glass and designer made jewellery.

www.artifex.co.uk
Tel. 0121 323 3776

Artifex
The Mitchells
Weeford rd
Sutton Coldfield
B75 6NA

**The stories in this book are inspired by the music of the same name, which is available on the CD and LP Scattered Chapters.
Released by and available from Psychotron Records.**

Starfield
Scattered Chapters
Nordkapp
One For Billie
Sharing Days
A Cottingley Secret
Through Braden's Door
The Constant Friend
The Kissing Gate
Requiem
She Who Gently Smiles
The Work Of Angels
The Stars Look Down On Linda
The Wounded Healer
Turning Earth
Precious
The Melody Weaver's Son
Heartsong

Music created by Gordon Giltrap and Paul Ward.
All guitars: Gordon Giltrap.
Keyboards synthesisers and programming: Paul Ward.
All tracks produced mixed and mastered by Paul Ward.
Published by Bucks Music.

John Devine: Uilleann Pipes and Whistles on The Wounded Healer and Heartsong.
Ian Mosely: Drums on Turning Earth.
Jenny Hanley: Spoken word on Precious.
Rod Edward's: Keyboard on Through Braden's Door.

Special thanks to Hilary Giltrap and Kathryn Ward for ongoing love and support, also profound words of encouragement from Pete Townshend.

CD Cover   CD Back

Blandine Anderson **Starfield**

Stoneware Sculpture
92 cm high by 24 cm wide by 42cm deep

Starfield

Starfield lies on the very edge of the ever-expanding universe and every quarter of a second another star comes to rest there. It's bewildering! These tiny lights expanding ever outwards into the void — into nothingness. There would be sound if there was anything to vibrate between the tiny stars, but at least each star can hear its own sound. If a space traveller could reach this place after travelling for billions of light years, they might hear something as they passed through the Field and brushed against these filaments of energy. A gentle hum, maybe, or a series of harmonics. Perhaps they would feel the sound rather than hear it. The never-ending harmony of so many pinpoints singing together like the celestial choirs imagined by the religious, but actually unimaginable because infinity is only perceptible to the human brain for a split second, and this music goes on for ever. Perhaps the space traveller would outpace the ever-expanding field of stars and find himself in the void, wondering what he had actually heard and whether he had heard it at all. But he would remember the joy of that time as he passed through. The restfulness and creativeness of that place with all those stars flowing, changing place in an endless dance.

I look up at the stars and think how infinite in time and space they are. Myself a tiny dot in the history of the universe. And yet what a mystery that I seem to be able to hold a whole galaxy in my mind for a brief moment. Then it's gone to a remote corner of my brain to be replaced by unlocking a door to my own tiny world — my shed. But I am smaller than my shed, and that remembered galaxy is smaller than me. The universe surrounds my shed and my shed surrounds me, but if I close my eyes I can see my shed and the closest parts of the universe there, inside me. What a mystery. Is everything inside out — outside in? My big toe contains a galaxy of tiny subatomic particles. If I was small enough to travel through my toe in a space ship and see the stars and planets that go to make up my toe, I would feel like I was in a new universe — the universe of myself.

I go back outside and look at the stars again. They have faded, as dark blue sky replaces black, and have been replaced by a sickle moon resting on its back. The moon looks small above the looming dark shape of my house but I know it is massively bigger. The tiny pinprick stars, that I can still see, are massively bigger than the moon itself and this goes on, seemingly for ever. And yet, I can close my eyes and see it all inside me. Infinite mind. Tiny soul — so small that we cannot see it. We can only see from it.

From a distance Starfield might seem like a jumble of crammed-in lights — a mess of tangled dots. But it's not like that. If you could look closely you would see that each star has its own space. Not lined up in

Verso

ranks like the white crosses at the war memorial at Verdun but slowly shifting in relation to each other. And if you could listen to each one separately you would hear that it has a unique voice, a unique song. And each song would be more than enough to carry you through your life. Now the strange thing is, that although Starfield is at the edge of the universe, as far away from you as you could possibly imagine, it is, by some curious shape of the cosmos, as close as anything could be. This Field is inside us, and joins us to others who would search for meaning and understanding as we pass through our short-endless lives on one tiny planet. If we listen, we know those stars are there and that some, maybe one or two, have particular meaning to us. We recognise their songs — they are close to our own songs, if we have discovered them — and they comfort us.

I walk out and look up at the sky. The stars have gone, but on the grass in front of me, I see lain out at my feet, the Star Field. The souls of the loved ones that I thought I had lost forever are there now, close at hand but infinitely far away at the same time.

Detail

Scattered Chapters   11

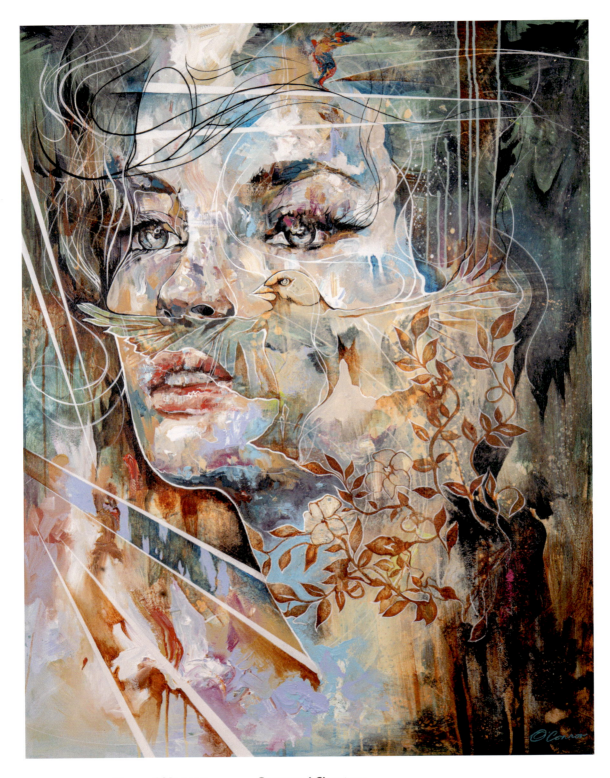

Danny O´Connor   **Scattered Chapters**

Mixed media on Canvas
92 cm by 122 cm
Signed O´Connor (lower right)

Scattered Chapters

Have you ever wondered whether the house you live in changes round you, to accommodate you, or if you change the way you are or even look because of the house you live in? This struck me as I stood on the top step of our bonkers 17th Century house looking up at a wonderful mural of crazy (and, I suspect, ecological) paintings by the 20th Century artist John French, and down at my wizardly spiritual clothing.

Our house is being decorated at the moment and the bones of it are being laid bare as we install our taste in colour on its ancient walls. Or is it the other way round — are we finding the colours that fit its taste? The rooms are crazy with bent and creaking beams and floorboards — rooms that you go through to get to other rooms. Not a convenient house but one that sprang into being and grew as the centuries moved on. Even though it's not very big, people can get lost in this house: we had a digeridoo player who came to stay here once, he worked as a guide for the National Trust, but he couldn't find his way out of our house! I should mention here that Gordon and Hilary Giltrap have stayed with us many times and have never got lost. Perhaps their wizardly-spirituality guides them through...

When Gordon first phoned me with the suggestion that I write a book based on the album that he was developing with composer and music-engineer par excellence, Paul Ward, I wondered what on earth I was going to write. Then he told me that a piece he had unearthed from several years back now had the title *Scattered Chapters*, and that he wondered whether that would be a good title for the book. When I told my wife, Judith, she said she thought that it was one of the best book titles she'd ever heard and that she wished she'd thought of it for her own writing!

Gordon told me that the reason he and Paul had come up with the idea of creating a book as well as an album was because they felt there was a story embedded in all the titles of the tunes — themes that ran through connecting all the tracks and demanding more than simple album notes. Looking through the titles and the stories that lay behind the music, I could see that the themes were related to the meaning of life and death, love and nature, spirituality and what lies beyond our normal experience. *Scattered Chapters* was the perfect excuse to explore all these ideas and see what happened. A bit like throwing paint at the wall and seeing how it turns out — a way of working that I employed to get past creative blocks when I was a film music composer (I described it in an interview for Rebecca Seal's book, *Solo*) and, in the case of *Scattered Chapters,* it worked!

Ideas sprang out of nowhere. Things I'd never thought of became real on the page. Love stories happened by chance. People I'd never met rose to greet me, and in the centre, like the hub of a wheel, was the story *The Melody Weaver's Son*. This track was originally a tribute to Gordon's friend and mentor Del Newman — he saw him as a father figure guiding him through such iconic albums as *Troubadour*. But the more Gordon thought about the piece and the sentiment behind it, the more he realised that it had many levels and could indeed apply to his son Jamie, who died so suddenly and left us wondering what life was all about, and that was when it evolved into its final title. So naturally, following Gordon's ideas of Teacher and Pupil, Guru and Devotee, Father and Son, my story was inspired by Jamie. As in this story and on the entire album, Jamie lives on in music and words. He lives on in a beautiful guitar design. And he lives on in our hearts in a way that I would never have thought possible.

I have struggled with the idea that the one inevitable thing in life is that I will die one day. In these pages, I have explored possibilities of what happens next. Biblical Heaven and Hell have been written about plenty of times over the past millennia, as have Reincarnation, Karma and getting off the cycle of life and death to attain Nirvana. But other ideas of what we are and what the energy is that makes us conscious, and whether it can be wiped out at death or perhaps continue in a different form, are all being explored now. From the healer and Shaman to the subatomic physicist, discoveries, ideas and beliefs, theories and practices, all abound.

I wrote *Scattered Chapters* in a certain order that made sense to me at the time. It is very likely that the order is now changed to suit the flow of the music to which this book is so surely attached. That will be an interesting experiment!

Way back in the 1970s, I went on a Gulbenkian music and choreography summer school, and at the end of the course, the tutors asked choreographers and composers to create separately with no knowledge of each other's work. At the final performance, music and dance came together in a completely unplanned way, and what was so amazing was how well it worked and how much we discovered.

I trust that the same will happen here, in fact I'm sure it will! I have a great belief in the magic of chance (in fact it's sprinkled liberally throughout these chapters, so whatever stream of consciousness I was following when I wrote one story after another, having planned the order myself, I am sure that how it all turns out will be as it was meant to be.)

If you want to see my original order you can go to my website www.wordandnote.com so that you can see how all the stories developed one from another... or you can choose not to... it's your book now!

Val Pitchford   **Nordkapp**

Oil on Canvas
52 cm by 82 cm
Signed V. Pitchford (lower left)

Nordkapp

We stood on the edge of the sea, the edge of the world, the edge of the sky and watched the matter that we had been waiting for, longing for, reach our planet and dance with earth's own familiar atoms. Slowly, it seemed, the soundless vision grew to fill everything. There was a music in our souls and our minds and it made us stop and stare, with open mouths in the freezing cold, at an endless unfolding of space as it met our solid earth. That solar wind had travelled ninety-three million miles to reach us — a wind that crossed space causing untold events — affecting everything in its path. It brought news of other places so distant, that we could only guess through mathematics what had happened there and watch it unfold in a slow dance that we could not understand. We wanted to leap off the edge and into the cosmos but we could not, being hampered by our own gravity that held us so firmly to our own planet's floor. Spinning round, we tried to dance with the green sky, but we were separated by such distance we couldn't feel it, we couldn't hear it, we could only watch, dizzy with awe.

It was 2002 and I took my sons to Glastonbury. For the first time, I understood the reason for amplified music, for light shows, for huge crowds listening to tiny people on a distant stage. It was Coldplay, it was Politik, and the music hit us — a wave of sound hitting our bodies and making us vibrate. The sky above was filled with aurora-like images and colours. The effect was to make us feel completely connected to the music being made by the tiny distant people on that stage. So many of us in such a huge space but every one of us vibrating like a hundred thousand tuning forks in a field of grass. Gradually the music subsided leaving us empty and clean. Silence, then a roar of many appreciations. Then more, then more. But in the midst we felt still, motionless, caught in the spell of the hugeness of such an experience.

Afterwards, the beer flowed, and the crowds flowed away, leaving us to look at the massive speaker towers that stood high above us in ranks up the hill, and I understood what sound can do.

To see vibration but not hear it was strange to us then. It was only afterwards that we discovered that we had heard music coming from inside our heads. It was impossible to explain to each other exactly what we had heard, but it seemed that there was a common thread of imagined sound that ran through all of us. A common bond of human imagination that connected every man woman and child of every race creed or colour together in one tiny place on one tiny planet in a vast universe. To make this music, to find it again, may be the beginning of all music. A need to make sense of what is seen but cannot be heard, what is in our heads but has no words. Perhaps we must make music to match the endless mystery of the cosmos both outside and inside us.

And that is where it all started.

Roy Meats   **One for Billie**

Acrylic on board
61 cm by 61 cm
Signed Roy Meats (lower right)

One for Billie

This girl sought to care. When she was young and too small to care for the people around her, though she would love to have done so, she cared for her dollies, she cared for her soft toys and particularly an old, battered donkey with one eye. The donkey was small and stiff and had a sad demeanour that needed cheering up. Cheering things up was what this girl was especially good at. She cheered up the doors, the walls, the windows of the house. She cheered up the carpets, the skirting boards, and the chair legs. And every now and then she would get the chance to cheer up a person.

As she got older, her chances to care for actual people came her way. She had younger siblings to look after – mend their toys, heal their grazed knees, comfort them after a nightmare, protect them from thunderstorms. She had elderly grandparents to listen to as they told their stories, often repeatedly; as they complained of lumbago or arthritis; as they feared for their future and that of their country. She honed and shaped her skill of caring and cheering until she was old enough to leave her home and join with another person to create a family of her own. A family to love.

But that was when the trouble started. The one person that she wanted to care for and bring cheer to couldn't receive it. He moved away from her on a different path and they inevitably found themselves in different worlds. True, her children were there for her to cherish and protect, and that gave some kind of link to her husband – their father. But it was not enough – she couldn't get through to him, she couldn't reach him. And eventually he left her life altogether.

With all this caring and cheering she gave out, she found that she needed some for herself. But there was nobody. Would she become empty she wondered, unable to give out anymore, unable to provide the vital love-energy that her children needed?

The music did it for her. She didn't play but she listened. She had always sung and she could carry the music that she heard around in her voice. It was a cheerful sound and it made all around her cheerful. The music she heard enfolded her in its arms and carried her on through the difficulties of life in a way that was almost magical.

There was a man who made music like no other. When she heard him play it was as if he knew the inside of her head and what she most needed. She went to his concerts when she could and sat right at the front, admiring his dexterity, soaking in his spirit as his music whirled round inside her head, healing, healing, healing. Her life with her children went on but he never knew the support that he'd given. On stage, blinded by lights, he caught glimpses of of a gentle face, but no more.

He played.

She listened.

She cared and cheered her children through their single-parent lives.

Scattered Chapters   19

Then one evening, as he walked off the front of the stage to meet some friends in the audience, he stumbled right in front of her. She automatically put out her hand to steady him and their eyes met. What flowed between them at that moment was the energy of two worlds, worlds that fitted so well:

He needed her care.
She needed his music.
He needed to give her music.
She needed to care for him.

And their bright light shone — two dazzling planets. But not just for each other — for those around them — cared for, music inspired, loved.

Detail

Detail

Scattered Chapters 21

Emma Wood **Sharing Days**
Fused Glass
66 cm by 66 cm

Sharing Days

At the end of the day, when all's said and done, and push comes to shove, like, it was truly a sharing day. And if anyone gainsay it, I'll give them a sharp rap on the kneecap with me tuning fork — it's an 'A' you know. Not that I use it anymore. Not now I've got this little electronic gizmo that tells me when I'm in tune.

Now tuning, there's a mystery. You know, some old geezer called Stravinsky said that harpists spend ninety percent of the time tuning their harps and the other, what, ten percent playing out of tune. Ha, he was a funny cove and no mistake — he wrote this Rite or something for a dance that was so rude that even the French couldn't take it and it started a riot. Mind you, the piece became famous later 'cos Disney used it in *Fantasia* — must have been some good after all.

But to get back to tuning, there's a joke: this man is about to be executed by firing squad and is asked if he has any final request and he says, now mark my words, he says 'can I tune my banjo first?' God knows where he got the banjo from at this point, out in the desert or wherever in the middle of nowhere, but anyway he gets his banjo out and starts to tune it, but he never finishes, and I hear you say, 'the firing squad couldn't stand the noise and shot him anyway,' but that's not what happened, no, he didn't finish because YOU CAN'T TUNE A BANJO! EVER!

Notwithstanding, I like that word. Dickens uses it a lot, you know. I don't really know what it means... my wife says it's something like 'in spite of'. She's probably right — usually is about that sort of thing. Notwithstanding... now where was I? I'm not ready to finish with this tuning lark, yet: so I've got this tuning gizmo and it tells me when I'm too sharp or flat by showing a little red line above or below the note name (you do have to know which note you're going for or it doesn't work at all) and when you've got it right it shows a little green line. Then you're right to go — green light! But what I wonder is, was that note really in tune or did I believe it was because the little gizmo told me it was? Am I just going around playing this guitar and everyone's saying to themselves 'ugh, that sounds horrible,' but I'm saying to myself, 'oh, the beauty of my in-tune guitar, everyone loves it so!' But, now this is where the real magic comes in: Apparently, they all believe I'm in tune too!

Notwithstanding my rabbiting on about tuning, (and I make no apology as tuning is the first and very necessary part of a sharing day) (and I make no apology for using the word notwithstanding, possibly wrongly, 'cos I like it) we definitely shared that day.

There was the food!

Nobody knew where it came from.

I turned up with me Walkers salt 'n' vinegar and a small sausage roll. Wife said, 'you'll need more than that!' She was right, usually is about that sort of thing.

Well, anyway, I wasn't the only one hoping I could cadge a sarnie off one of me guitar-playing neighbours. Seems we all were! And after a morning of tuning and finger exercises and trying to read tabs and whatnot, we were starving! Literally, I mean, starving. And there was no way I was going to get through the rest of the day on a packet of crisps and a tiny sausage roll, especially as I'd already had them for my elevenses!

But somebody came in and said there was this food. They didn't know where it came from but there it was, laid out in the kitchen. There was mackerel pâté and all these little French loaves and tomato soup to dip them in. There was cheese, not ordinary cheese, really stinky ripe cheese! With pickles! There was fruit! (*Good* for you, the wife would say!) and to drink there was water or even red wine. Well, I had a small glass of the wine and no more, cos I had to drive home, but when I went on to have water, it tasted even better than the wine. Imagine that!

So we sat round and ate this lovely food and talked and shared stories about guitars we'd known and how we got such and such a riff off some amazing celeb. We talked about our nails, about our children, about the books we read, about politics and religion. (Yes I know you're not supposed to talk about politics and religion at the dinner table but somehow, though we didn't all have the same views, we managed to discuss things in a truly amicable way... notwithstanding). It was strange. It was wonderful! Somehow this food and drink reached more parts of us than just our tummies.

Now I didn't come to the sharing day looking for love — I've got plenty of that at home, I'm a lucky man — but I found a love that I didn't expect to find. You might call it friendship, or comradeship, mateyness, but I'd call it love. Not that I wanted go around kissing all my beardy fellow guitarists! No, it was more than that. A great swelling of warmth inside. A moist eye and a big smile that said, 'I don't care who you are or what you believe, here's a bit of love I want to share with you.'

Well, you can imagine there was a bit of hugging after that meal and then we were treated to a performance by a friend of our teacher. He played some Irish — I like a bit of Irish, and it all sounded so smooth and confident that I dozed off. Only woke up with the applause at the end!

'Good?' I asked my neighbouring guitarist, who'd dug me in the ribs to wake me up.

'Good!' he said.

So after our little treat-sleep-performance, it was time for us to start playing that piece we'd all come to learn from the source, himself.

'Heartsong.'

Well, you can imagine how it all started off. Everyone knew it slightly differently so we clattered along for a bit and then stopped, and listened to the maestro, and tried a few things. And started again. Better this time, but it sounded a bit like an audio version of a ripe cheese. Riper even, than the cheeses at that mysterious lunch, cos we'd all gone out of tune.

So we all tuned up on our little gizmos!

It sounded better the third time, notwithstanding the fact that we needed to tune again. And this time I made an amazing discovery: if I tuned with my gizmo and then *listened* to everyone else and *tweaked* it a tiny, tiny bit. It sounded even better.

Imagine 'Heartsong' with twenty guitars, all in tune with each other, all listening, all playing from the heart and you will hear a music so full, so warm that you will float out on it — you'll find that you can fly.

When I'd hugged everyone and sworn continued contact with everyone and said goodbye to everyone, I walked out to my car with a new tune in my ear. Warm, affectionate, it was; it paused, it rose, it blossomed; it came and it went. And it was only years later that I heard him play 'Sharing Days.'

Detail

Jan Gay **A Cottingley Secret (triptych)**
Mixed Media on board
64 cm by 41 cm
Signed Jan Gay (first board lower right)

A Cottingley Secret

That young girl could feel the shadows of her garden coming out to meet her. The world slipped by under her feet as the groundswell of tiny creatures ebbed and flowed in a rhythm of nature. She could feel the sway of trees, the groaning of roots, the air from Africa, and the sun, which was millions of miles away, sent its beams down to warm her hair. Everything was alive then, everything was vibrant, and imagination lived in the same world as the forces of the universe — inside her head. She twirled and set motes of dust fairies dancing and jumping in the rays of light that shone down to make shadows in the grass. The world was her peace then. Nature had no fear of her nor she of it. In that moment she was one — mind and body fused — a tiny vibration in the vastness of the universe.

Later on, another world came and would not leave her alone. Parents and 'people that knew' told her that she must learn narrow facts, earn money, become famous. Become, in fact, a great big lump of made-up-ness instead of being a tiny vibration that had its place flowing in the 'ten thousand things'. She lost her sense of the truth around her. She couldn't feel the vibrant earth beneath her feet or see the moment-by-moment change of everything around her. Now, the world was fixed.

Firmly.

In her hand.

Great and famous people admired and listened to her, she and they both beguiled by a fantasy that spoke of wealth and magic. She couldn't see the real magic of the universe, only the made-up magic of somebody else's limited imagination. She played and danced in this world, refusing to see what she had lost and counting all this wealth and attention, fame and fortune, as so much better than her true place in the cosmos.

Now she is old and she can see again, even though her sight is failing. Her worlds meet and her hands feel the breeze from Timbuctoo. Truth, truth, the truth she told and the truth set her free. The world of fame and fortune dropped her like a stone and she was left with... nothing. Nothing but the relief of not living a lie anymore, and a world that came back to her with open arms. Her gnarled arthritic feet danced on the grass again and her stiff distorted hands reached out to touch the petals of a rose. Her mind, clear of lies and deceit, of guilt and fear, could allow the world back in, and the world could live through her. Happy, happy in her oneness, she breathed, knowing the value of life and the short sweetness of it, and knowing that she was a small vibration, a moonbeam, that would soon join the rest of the universe.

Trudy Good **Through Braden´s Door**
Oil on Canvas
62 cm by 82 cm
Signed TMG (lower right)

Through Braden's Door

You peek through the gap left by the open door and see him. He is small. He is yours. He is himself already. He has picked up a guitar that seems big for him even though it is only three-quarter size, but he is making sounds on it. More than sounds — music. More than music — his music. His nimble hands are not strong, but they are determined. They already know their path, predestined, it seems as though some god has kissed him and left a gift behind. A gift of music.

Note follows note. Falters at times but always finds its direction again. He doesn't know anyone is watching. He is totally absorbed, unselfconscious. A place that every performer would like to be. His music is not virtuosic, it is pungent, visceral. It slowly pulls you in as you listen more and more. In fact, the more you listen, the more you sense the fact that these are not random notes, no more than a child's drawing is a random scribble. The music has unconscious form that is taking shape in front of you. Then you notice he repeats a phrase, then another, then another. This is not boring, it is lulling, lulling you into a world of no time, no space, just him and you and this music.

The smell as she returned to the kitchen was of burning rice. It was not a kind smell. It made her feel a failure. Wasted food. Wasted time. And she would have to try and rescue the pan by plunging it in warm water and find another one to cook some more rice in. Tea would be late too. Her children would be over-hungry, grumpy and difficult to put to bed. Oh why, why did she have to lose concentration? Why couldn't she just have left her boy to get on with his music and concentrate on looking after her little family?

It was hard on her own. She found some more rice in a packet at the back of the cupboard. The meatballs would be alright in the bottom oven. They'd be a little late but it doesn't matter, she said to herself, doesn't matter. Then she buried her head in a tea towel and wept.

Tea. Make yourself some tea, somebody who cared had told her. She put the rice on and boiled the kettle — just a little water — to make a cuppa. But she knew he'd have made it better so she had another cry as the teabag soaked.

By some magic the tea tasted really good, just like his. And she sipped it gratefully. Grateful that she'd known him, shared his life.

You can't help yourself. You have to go back and see how your little boy's getting on with his guitar. The door is still slightly open. Take a peek. He's stopped — the guitar is still straddled across his lap. You sip your tea

and just watch. He says something you can't hear. He's talking to himself but it's so quiet. You want to go in then and hug him. Say you're sorry. You take another sip of tea and prepare to cross the threshold.

At that moment he starts to play and you recognise it. You're sure you do. Then you're wondering whether it was because you listened so intently to him a short while ago, or he'd picked up a tune that you'd both heard someone else play.

You don't know. But does it matter? He's made it his own wherever it came from. You notice now that it has more form. You can almost anticipate the next phrase. The repeats are more regular somehow. Everything's firmer, more defined. It's like he has remembered the pith of the music, the bones. But you miss the adventure, the not-knowingness of earlier. To discover or even uncover music for the first time always seems like magic.

Detail

Detail

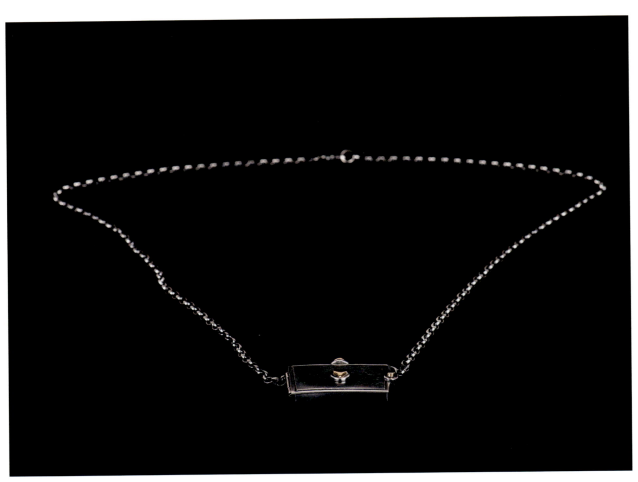

Nick Hubbard Studio **The Constant Friend**
Solid Silver Pendant

The Constant Friend

Without you, I am simply a beautiful object stuck away in a dark box or standing, leant against the wall, or worst of all, hanging from the wall like some kind of trophy. True, if you see me, you might like my shape with my elegant waist, my long black neck, my small head emblazoned with my maker's name. My wood might attract you: my gracefully curved sides made of a dark reddish-brown rosewood with its beautiful grain running the length of my body; my front made from cedar with a straight grain that is narrow from slow growth. If you look at the grain close-up, you might see time and multiple universes reflected in the wood. And if you look at my black ebony fingerboard supported by strong mahogany, you might see how it is elegantly shaped and crafted to suit your hand if you cared to play me. And if you bothered to pick me up and turn me round you would find that same rosewood on my back, displaying even more spectacular grain, swirling and glinting in the light — a still pool of potential sound.

But there will be no sound unless you pick me up and play me, so my job is to tempt you, lure you, and then keep you coming back for more. I must respond immediately, even though I know, and you know, that the more you make my sound, the better it becomes.

I have never ceased to wonder at the sound he makes. It doesn't seem to matter which guitar he plays — and they all sound different in their own uniqueness — *his* sound is there too, a matchless warmth and depth. I have filmed him many times, looked back at his playing in close detail, but I still can't fathom what makes his sound. Is it his totally individual way of plucking the strings? His left hand and the way it stretches with such strength? His choice of melody line — the fact that it is his own music, always his own music? His careful use of electronics to amplify and change the tone of the guitar?

He builds his sound as if it were a wall — every brick thought about, every join carefully fitted and sealed together with musical sand and mortar. But even at the building-site of his playing the sound is beautiful. I listen close sometimes, without any electronics between me and his sound, and it is crisp, clear, the perfect start for a journey out into a vast space, whether a hall, church, over the Internet, on a record. In the beginning is his sound, *his* sound, and I often wonder how a guitar must feel when he picks it up to play. He has many guitars — are they jealously jostling to get his attention? 'Ah,' one may say. 'At last you find me, master.'

And in his hands I play. Today, he has chosen me. Today I will be his friend. But I notice sadness in his hands, a gentleness, a soulfulness, that I haven't felt before. He is almost hesitant for a moment and then plunges into a music of grief. For this, I must give him my full range, from low to

high, from quiet to loud, from soft to hard, and all the endless gradations between.

'I will be your solace, your constant friend, today. I will feel what you want and give you sounds that you seek.'

And as we make this music, I think of the saddest thing I ever knew — that humans could turn on each other and take their humanity away, and eventually, their lives. The horror of that holocaust will always remain in the bones of the saddest music. But, although I feel sad that anyone could lose their love enough to commit such premeditated murder on such a massive scale, it is the victims that move me so. Those lives brought slowly, deliberately, to an end in an inhuman factory of fear. To see the hopelessness of their situation but to see the hope in their warm, human faces is so sad — it is the saddest thing. Then second saddest is the way those people, so awfully treated, should then treat another nation so badly, so inhumanly. We don't seem to learn but carry on the relentless destruction of others through our fear.

But wait, I have missed something. This music is not a grieving for many but for one person. On a personal level there is another saddest thing. If I can just step out of my historic grief and listen.

The loss of a child.

For no reason.

No lack of love on anyone's part.

Just loss.

On close up, this is the saddest thing. There is no answer to this.

But again, wait: in the music that my friend makes I can hear the birth of a new guitar — one made from mahogany. And at the twelfth fret, the letters JG.

So, out of this heart-breaking, meaningless death something good can come. Not the destruction of others out of fear but a new instrument of beauty — a memory of love that will last.

And I promise that I will not be jealous or fractious anymore, as I wait for you to play me. I *will* be your constant friend.

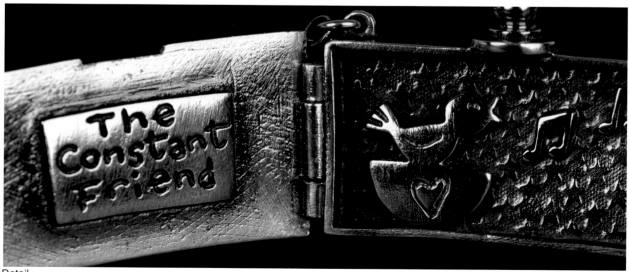

Detail

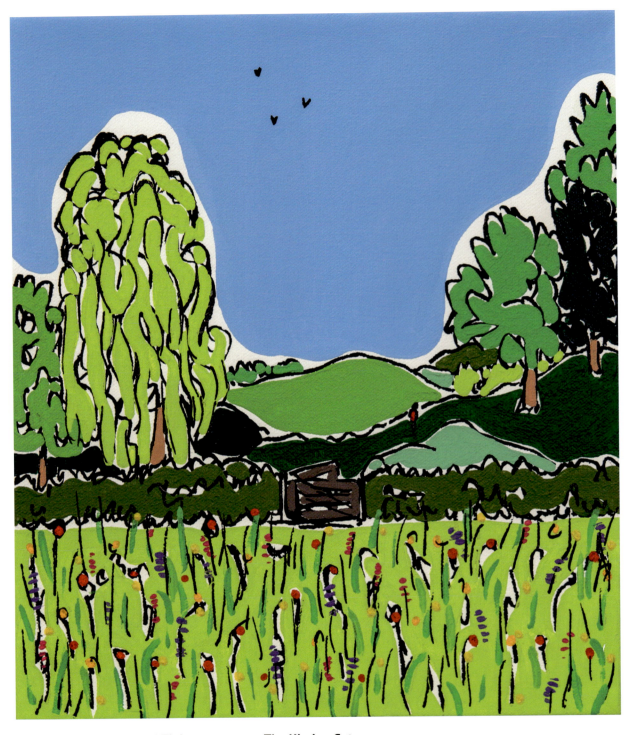

Rachel Tighe   **The Kissing Gate**

Acrylic on Canvas
26 cm by 31 cm

The Kissing Gate

You weren't what I was expecting.

For such a long time I had been single, waiting for 'the right one'. Friends had married, had children, divorced, got married again while I still waited, reluctant to step on the dance floor of intimate relationship. I had one, oh yes, one. I gave my all and got my heart broken but that was a long time ago.

I live on the edge of suburbia, but a block away from open fields and rolling countryside. And most days I go for for a walk and, being a routine sort of person, I always walk the same way, knowing that it will take fifty-five minutes precisely. That is, unless I meet someone I know and stop for a chat, which is rare as I don't know many people in this sprawling suburbia. True, I recognise fellow walkers who take that same route but in the opposite direction and have their own routine of say, walking for fifty-six minutes, or perhaps forty-three-and-a-half minutes. Whatever, I always meet them at different stages on my walk and we always nod in acknowledgement of each other's existence, but that is it. No conversation. No spoiling our routine.

It was spring and one morning, having read *The Wind in the Willows* to get myself to sleep the night before, I found myself inspired by the Mole who said something like 'stuff spring cleaning for a bunch of bananas' — that's not what he said but what I felt about what he said — and I decided to take a different walk. Take time. Pack a rucksack with waterproof and sandwiches and beer. Have a day off.

I looked at the map and decided to take a path I'd never taken before, 'the path less travelled', I said to myself with humorous hope.

It had rained in the night and the morning sun brought steam off the grass. The path I took was unexpected and slippery. It took me down dark tunnels of tree-lined and leafroofed paths that must have been walked for centuries. Then with a flash of light, out into open meadows and grand English scenery which brought the theme tune to the *Vicar of Dibley* into my mind.

I got caught up in thoughts of 'will I ever find someone?' or 'will she have been married before and have children and would I want that?' or 'what will she look like? Blonde? Dark? Tall? Short? Plump? Athletic?' 'The trouble is', I reflected, 'that I'm so shy, I wouldn't know what to say if I did meet the 'right one', and she would slip away, out of my grasp, leaving me to muse on how I had lost the only person that I was meant to be with.'

I was so caught up in my thoughts that I didn't notice the beautiful rolling countryside around me and failed to spot the kissing gate until I was automatically going through it and nearly collided with someone coming through it from the other side. I found myself looking straight into the face of a woman with a snub nose, freckles, and blue eyes that sparkled in amusement. She was the same height as me and wearing a

Scattered Chapters   37

green woollen hat which covered her hair.

'Sorry,' we both said at the same time — a short chorus which continued with: 'I was just... caught up in my thoughts.'

We smiled, caught up, as we were now, in an intimate situation, stuck, as we were, in fact wedged by our rucksacks and forced into a close dance, the outer railing encircling us and the gate itself stuck between us.

'Well, this is really funny,' she giggled. 'How do we get out of this?'

I laughed too, but to cover my embarrassment. She seemed much bolder than me, much more confident.

I moved one way but she did the same, bringing us even closer. I could smell her toothpaste and the thought came to me that I was so glad I'd cleaned my teeth thoroughly that morning and not snacked on a cheese sandwich on the way. I tried to move back out into the opening but found that my rucksack had snagged on the railing behind me. She did the same with the same result.

'I can't turn round,' she said.

'Neither can I,' I replied.

'I'll just have to reach over and release your bag, then you can go back and I can come through.' And without waiting for an answer she put one arm round me, brushing her cheek against mine, and with a bit of pushing she managed to free my bag from the railing and I could walk backwards out of the gate.

'Thankyou,' I said, shamefacedly.

'De nada,' she replied as she walked past me and on down the path.

'De what?' I called after her.

'De nada. It's Spanish for 'it's nothing'.'

And with that she was gone.

But it wasn't nothing to me. It was the most intimate moment I'd had for many years. It meant so much to me, not 'nothing'. She had come close to me and in that moment a spark of recognition had passed between us, or was it just my imagination? Somehow, she felt right — right for me. But I knew nothing about her except that she was resourceful, confident and humorous — things that I sometimes felt I lacked. I hoped to see her again but that might be the only time she walked down this path. It wouldn't be the only time that I did.

Once a week, when I had a day that was freer from work, I would take that route. I grew to love it. The whole walk took four hours and took me through woodland meadows and dark lanes. Over streams and rivers and past old broken-down barns and curious outbuildings. I thought of her and our close encounter and how the longer time went on, the more certain I was that she was 'the right one.' But this is silly, I said to myself. How could I know from that brief encounter?

Every time I got to the kissing gate I paused, wondering if I would see her coming the other way and imagining coming up with a friendly greeting that would bring us into conversation. One hot summer's day I paused for a drink of water and decided to sit down by the path and gaze over the meadow below me. There were poppies and wildflowers in abundance. The farmer, evidently, had decided to allow his land to grow, free of chemicals, and let the wild back in. I loved it and was so absorbed in watching the dance of swaying plants in the gentle breeze and butterflies fluttering to and fro that I didn't hear the creak of the gate behind me.

'Hullo,' said a voice that I recognised. 'Beautiful, isn't it. Do you mind?' And she sat down beside me, the woman that I had been wondering about for weeks.

'N...no, not at all,' I stammered. 'P...please feel free.' She had already felt free, so my invitation was somewhat pointless. It made me laugh and I continued by putting out my hand.

'Jon,' I said. 'Short for Jonathan.'

'Sam,' she said, taking my hand in a firm grip and shaking it. 'Short for Samantha. I was wondering whether I'd see you again. It seemed like I should have said something. I felt as though I'd been a bit... you know... rude, just brushing past you like that. Truth was, I was in a hurry to get back to work.'

'That's alright, you weren't rude at all. You handled the situation much better than me.' I blushed at this point, couldn't help it — the curse of fair skin. 'If it had been up to me we'd still be there now...' Then I juddered to a halt, realising how that sounded. 'I mean...'

'I know what you mean,' she said, laughing.

'Yes, well, and anyway,' I wanted desperately to get away from my mistaken flirting. 'What work were you getting back to?'

'I'm a pet food nutritionist!' she announced, and then laughed.

'A pet food nutritionist?' I asked, wondering whether she wore a net over her short brown hair as she prodded pieces of Chappie with a scalpel.

'No, just kidding,' she laughed. 'People always ask me what I do at parties and when I tell them I'm a mathematician their eyes glaze over and they change the subject.'

'But maths is the basis of what *I* do,' I said.

'And what's that?' she asked.

'I write music.'

'You're a composer! How illustrious!'

'I wouldn't call it illustrious, I just write bits of music for documentaries.'

'What? TV documentaries? You're on TV? I've probably heard your music. I love documentaries!' She smiled and her blue eyes twinkled in her weathered freckled face.

'Well, you might have heard something, I suppose, although they mix my music so low, you probably wouldn't notice it.'

'What sort of docs do you write for?'

'Space, mainly. I seem to have hit a good sound for programmes about the cosmos. Very thin, slow, music. Not much to it really but I do get a lot of royalties per note. Like I said, you probably wouldn't even...'

'But that's thoroughly weird,' she interrupted. 'That's the area of maths that I work in. I'm working on a formula to find out what happens at the edge of the universe. It's taken me years already. Actually,' she added

enthusiastically. 'It was at the point at which we met at the kissing gate that I had an idea and had to rush home to get it down!'

'And has it worked?' I asked, thinking that was weeks ago.

'No, it will take a bit longer than that, years probably, but it was a turning point in my life as a mathematician.'

'It was a turning point in my life too.' I said it before I could stop myself.

'Really?' she smiled her amazing smile. 'Did you find the 'lost chord'?'

'Something like that,' I replied.

I dared to smile at her then. She smiled back and I wondered if she knew what I meant. Then we both turned and looked at the sunlit meadow below us. I could feel the electricity of her presence so close to me.

'It's funny,' she sighed. 'Doesn't that look like a field of stars to you?'

'Yes,' I said, as I imagined us going to a party together both pretending to be pet food nutritionists.

Detail

Blandine Anderson   **Requiem**
Stoneware Sculpture
41 cm high by 33 cm wide by 14cm deep

Requiem

I was expecting some sort of rushing down a tunnel but I wasn't expecting this: a giant mole. I read somewhere, before I started my death, that there *was* a mole and that he was *small*, but he made a big *difference*. This mole is BIG and he is INDIFFERENT, to me at least. I just seem to be following his posterior at great speed as he tunnels ever lower into the earth.

'Excuse me!' I shout at his great hairy hind legs, 'Where are we going?' But all that happens is that I think I said it, but no sound comes from me, as there is nothing to make the sound. I am just seeing and hearing but I have no arms or legs or lungs or mouth, and I can't *feel* the rough sides of the tunnel. There must be some kind of torch embedded in my eyes or perhaps it's my aura giving off a ghostly light — otherwise I wouldn't be able to see this hairy backside speeding along in front of me.

Perhaps I can stop? But no! I have no control over my physical progress down this hole. Oh, I can smell — so there must be a nose somewhere — the soil around me smells satisfactorily earthy. Nice! It's nice to be able to smell. But could I smell a moment ago or did I decide I could just now? I don't remember smelling anything since the smell of the carpet that I lay and died on.

We're still whizzing down this tunnel and I'm feeling cheated: wasn't there going to be eternal rest? Isn't that what Requiem Eterna means? Perhaps floating about in the stars, seeing the great cosmos spread out before me. Perhaps seeing God's purpose — although I half pretended to myself that I didn't believe in God, and I just looked at Him out of the corner of my eye — a sort of insurance policy, in case...

Funny how I said 'HE'! Did it automatically. I'm also assuming that I'm following a male mole down this hole.

Now I've lost my sense of time — how long has this been going on? Suddenly, yes SUDDENLY, I feel frightened. If I have no sense of time, then I might already have been following a giant mole for eternity! How would I *know*? Perhaps my thoughts will give me a clue. There may be no time *outside* me, but I might still have a sense of time *inside* me. So I'll hold onto that, and remember that I only recently got my sense of smell back, what, minutes ago?

We turn a corner and I feel something — was that something? A roughness where my shoulder should have been. But I have no shoulder — I am incorporeal! No body, just a sense or essence.

What's this? A sudden turn upwards. Did I feel a slight grazing of my feet, my knees? Anyway, we're going up and the giant mole is slowing down. Harder work, I guess. He, she, it, must have to work against gravity. What am I saying? Gravity? Could there be gravity? Here? I don't feel it. Up, up we go. And with that, hope.

Then it comes to me — I AM ALONE, except for this mole. No one else,

Scattered Chapters 43

Verso

no love, nothing but my own bodiless existence. I had forgotten all the love I had for others and the love that was returned. I am so glad that I have now remembered it, but at the same time I wish I hadn't. Where is my Requiem now? The endless sadness of love that I can *only* remember.

The mole is getting slower and I want to push its posterior. I want to be out in the light. There must be light up there, mustn't there? I try to push at the mole but just get a strange feeling of going into its body, and I don't like that feeling so I desist.

The mole is going very slowly now, but it's still moving upwards.

And now I'm hearing something new — it's like a hum reverberating through the earth above my head. A resonance that shifts downwards, then down again, then again... then up to where it started.

In my impatience to know what this sound is, I push at the mole's backside again, and again I find myself sinking into its body. It's an unpleasant sensation but I persevere to find out if I can see out of its eyes. After a ghastly struggle up through its intestines, heart, and lungs, I get as far as its head but all that I can see out of its eyes is darkness. There is one thought in its brain that I can detect, though: *Grub!*

I have had enough of this soul-curdling sensation and quickly make my way back out of its body. In the gloom behind I can still hear this humming pattern and it's getting louder. The mole still pushes its way up through the earth, slowly, forcefully, while I languish in the dark tunnel behind it, trying to deal with my feelings of love and loss. Is this purgatory? It's not hell... yet. 'Be hopeful', I say to myself, and the words *Negative Capability* come to mind. 'Wait and hope to see what will happen.'

As I remember these words, my soul lifts, and that's all of me now. Light begins to break through the darkness above and, at the same time, the reverberation that I was hearing turns into music. It is slow and sad and has weaving melodies of guitar. I know that style — it is close to me.

The mole stops for a moment and then scrambles up into the light. I float up past crevasses and rocks, the music gets louder and more powerful all the time. The sun is above me, and as I float higher, I see the mole eating something that wriggles, and down the hill from him, a meadow full of flowers. The land below me is gentle and free. Trees grow how they want to, grass is uncut and seedy, the wild vegetation is varied and colourful, and, for the first time, I realise that the mole is not a giant. The mole looks a perfectly normal size down there in the grass. No, it's me that is tiny — a vibration of energy — just spirit form, and the world down there is vast and beautiful.

And now I can sense other vibrations around me. I am not alone. We are many and in that crowd I might find him that I love, lost from each other as we were in the moment of death.

The music starts again, softly, insistently, growing to beauty and sadness and... I just caught it, a true happiness. I know what this is now, this music, it's *my* Requiem. And in this moment I realise that love and loss are inseparable but I would have it, yes I would have love, for all its pain!

Ann Pollard **She Who Gently Smiles**

Acrylic on Canvas
91 cm by 122 cm

She Who Gently Smiles

(A different angle on Dicken's Christmas Carol)

When I first found him in that horrible school, I knew then what he must have gone through. The place was cold, broken and cruel, and there was just him, just him, pacing the frozen classroom. He should have died but he was made of tougher stuff. He was all bone and sinew when I came to him. His face was stiff with cold, so stiff that he found it hard to smile as I reached up to embrace him, my dear, dear brother, and cover his cold cheeks with kisses as I told him the news: '**I have come to bring you home, dear brother!**'

He didn't seem to believe me to start with, so unexpected was my arrival on a post coach. So I clapped my hands and stroked his, hoping to warm him with my heart, my smile. As I looked round this desolate place I couldn't believe how cruel father had been to make him, my poor Eben, stay in this school, even at Christmas.

'**Father is so much kinder than he used to be,**' I started. Then told him of how we would have such a wonderful Christmas.

And Eben smiled.

The horrible and terrifying headmaster asked us into his best parlour for wine and cake. The wine tasted of vinegar, the cake of mud, so we took little and made haste to the front door and out to the chaise and made our way down the drive: **our quick wheels dashing the hoar frost and snow from off the dark leaves of the evergreens like spray**. We laughed and laughed with delight and joy until my brother stopped, his face suddenly looked grim. I wondered whether his heart had frozen at that moment and I hoped that mine would be big enough and warm enough to thaw it out.

'So, you say father has changed,' he said, looking out at the snowbound land as we travelled on. 'What do you mean by *changed?*' His voice had taken on an unfamiliar piercing tone and he would not look me in the eyes.

'Yes, he's so different, dear brother. He pays us attention, talks to us, spends time with mother and me, and lets mother buy nice things for us to eat. The house is warm now and there are no icicles on the inside of the windows.'

'And how do you know that he won't change back, little Fan? How do you know?' His look chilled me as he fixed me with a glare in his eyes that I had never seen before.

'I told you,' I replied, my heart beating faster. 'He said you're to be a man now.'

'A man?' my brother said. 'How do you know he won't cast me out of the house, throw me to the dogs? Eh? How do you know?'

Scattered Chapters

I started to cry and put my arm on his to pull him round to face me. 'Eben, my dear Eben, listen.' I implored between sobs. 'He said... he said you are to be prenticed to Mr Fezzywig. Y... you know, the lovely Mr Fezzywig with his cheerful wife and his beautiful daughters.'

'Ah, so...' was all the reply that I got and he looked down as though afraid to meet my tearful gaze. 'So, that's it. I will work for old Fezzywig.' He looked me full in the face then and worked his unaccustomed smile muscles into a grimace that was almost a smile. 'Fan, I hope that you're right and that father has changed for good.'

'He has, dear brother, he has.' My heart lifted then as I saw the warmth come back into his gaze. Our father had been so severe for so so long that I shouldn't be surprised, I told myself, that Eben found it hard to believe.

Our journey was more agreeable from then on as we caught the train down to London and talked of our hopes for Christmas and the future. I didn't see that cruel look in his eyes again, nor did I hear that piercing tone of voice. I thought then that I'd got my Ebenezer back, that his heart was good for life and that we could look forward to a merry future.

Father was good as his word and we *did* have a happy Christmas. Ebenezer put on a little weight and lost the skeletal edges in his face. He talked kindly to mother and me and respectfully to his father who often gave him the time of day. We were a happy family as we had never been before and I could see that my dear brother could hardly believe it at times and I never saw that grim look in his face as we danced and played our way through Christmastide.

After he went to work for Mr Fezzywig, I saw much less of him. He would drop in to see us at home and always had a kind word for 'his little Fan'. I knew that he had good times working for his first employer and that he was, in the main, happy. I also knew that he was on good terms with one of his employer's daughters, and that they walked out together. And I waited keenly to hear the news that they were betrothed to be married. But that news never came and he left Mr Fezzywig's employment 'for better things' he said. At that time I noticed a sly look come into his face from time to time, he became more secretive and told me little of what he was doing and what his actual way of earning a living was.

I fell in love with a joyful and handsome man — Charles. We were betrothed and were married and went to live in the city, not far from where my brother had newly set up his business. Ebenezer had few friends and rarely came to see us, even after my dear husband Charles died, he was little comfort and support to me and took scant interest in his little nephew, my only son, Fred.

I wondered what had happened to his heart. Had it hardened, due to the years of neglect that he had suffered when he was young? His face, when I saw him, had set into the grim look that I had so feared on the chaise ride from the school. The most I could hope for in a smile from him was a sly one. And I learnt that he had a new friend — money. Money was his all, his god, his child, his wife, his very life.

Money was what we needed too, but just simply to stay alive. After my dear Charles' death we were destitute and I went to him in his counting house and begged him to help us out. He didn't look at me; he didn't even call me by my name; all he had to say was:

'No, you have made your own bed and you must lie in it. I have paid good money to support the poor houses; you can go there.' Then he looked up, that sly smile on his face, and said, 'Of course, when your boy grows up, he may come and work for me then. But now,' he turn his face away. 'Go! Go!'

I cried and entreated him, not just for his money but for the sake of his soul, but he remained unmoved and I left, wondering when I would ever see him again, my poor lost Eben. I fell very ill for a while after that, but fortunately recovered, though it left me with a weakness. Although I knew that I was dead to him now — my brother, I made a vow that I would never give up hoping that he would change; that I would see, once again, the boy that I had rescued from that terrible school. And I vowed also that I would teach my son to do the same: never give up on him — to always be generous towards him.

Our fortunes improved, thanks to the generosity of my departed husband's cousin, George, who supported us and enabled Fred to get a good education. Time passed, and I didn't see Ebenezer, for I couldn't bear to look on the travesty of what he'd become. News came that he had a new friend, that money wasn't his only companion in life. Marley was his name, Jacob Marley, but my hopes for an improvement in his attitude were dashed when we heard that Scrooge and Marley were the most ruthless, cruel, money lenders in the city and were to be avoided like the plague if you had any sense.

In the meantime, my life was a happy one, though I was beset by illness and from time to time feared that I might not survive to see my son in safe employment and a happy family man. But there was something in me, a seed of hope, of optimism, that kept me going. My son would flourish; my brother would return from his early burial under the soil of cold, gold sovereigns to a full life.

Scrooge and Marley, Marley and Scrooge. The two sad rascals persisted in besmirching my family name, that is, until there was only one — Marley had died leaving my brother still awaiting redemption. Meanwhile, my son, Fred, grew strong and handsome and found himself a promising position in a charitable institution in the city. He payed occasional visits to his uncle Ebenezer and brought me news of his unchanged demeanour. My son found love and married and we all lived in a comfortable home together, but still my brother persisted in his mean ways and still I hoped and prayed for him.

It was a cold and bitter Christmas and I struggled with my health. The atmosphere in the streets was so thick that you could cut it with a knife. I kept inside and slept a lot. But one night I had a dream: I dreamed that 'Old Marley', a man who I had never set eyes upon, had returned from the grave to haunt my brother and set him free from his avaricious ways. Never mind my brother, the dream haunted me, and I encouraged Fred to go round and invite his uncle to join us for Christmas celebrations.

'Celebrations,' Fred retorted when he returned from his uncle's counting house. 'He doesn't know the meaning of the word and he wouldn't know a celebration if you dangled it in front of his long, frozen nose!'

'But you tried,' I said, gently smiling at him and putting my hand on his arm.

'I tried...'

'Well, perhaps this time, he will come,' I persisted.

'I doubt it. He gave me short shrift,' came the reply.

'Perhaps I should go...'

'No, mother. The cold and smog out there would kill you. You stay in... maybe he *will* come after all.'

I was certain that my dear son had said this to me to stop me from going out, hoping that the possibility of Ebenezer coming to celebrate Christmas with us would be enough. But it wasn't enough, and after Fred and his sweet wife had gone to bed, I stole out into the city of London in search of my brother. The streets were thick with a cold fog that came down like a yellow blanket. There was no freshness in the choking air, just the acrid smell of coal fumes and dust. I knew his chambers lay down a maze of alleys in a small dark court but I almost immediately got lost in the smoky labyrinth, finding it hard to see more than a few yards ahead. By a stroke of luck I spotted a hunched thin figure hastily making its way out of a dark tavern and I was sure it had my brother's shape and demeanour. I endeavoured to catch him up but he scuttled along so fast, and I found my breathing so difficult, that I had to be content to follow just fast enough to keep his dark figure in sight.

There was no one about as he entered the small dark yard where his chambers glowered above me like a faceless giant. He went through the gate ahead of me and paused at the door, longer than I expected, and I hoped to catch him then, before he entered. But he slipped furtively into the house without looking round. I opened the gate which shrieked with its pain of rust and grime and walked uncertainly up to the door. What would I ask him? How would I persuade him? I was so out of breath that I would hardly be able to speak and, on top of that, I had begun to feel the sickly sense of my ailment coming back to haunt me.

I paused at the door, gathering my wits, when a strange and ghastly thing occurred. The door knocker, which had been in the shape of a rusty old lion, changed into a face that I knew from my dream of the previous night. Old Marley. His face seemed empty of life, his eyes a misty yellow, his complexion a putrid red as though he had strangled himself by coming through the door like that. I nearly swooned there and then, but my life and death intention to save my brother held me up as I looked at the apparition in front of me.

'Go!' it said, its ghostly voice echoing round the buildings. A pale hand came through the door to push me away.

'I want to see my brother,' I said, standing my ground against this ghost.

'Go!' it cried again, louder this time, as though in pain. 'Leave him to me!'

I shook my head, though whether to say no to the ghost or to shake his existence out of my fevered mind, I don't know.

Another pale hand came out of the door and both hands pushed at my chest sending a chill right through my body. I fell back onto the ground and, as I scrambled up, the apparition's eyes that had been so misty and vague, gleamed at me like two lamps on a carriage.

'Leave him to me!' the ghastly voice insisted. 'Leave him to me!'

I turned then and stumbled away from the house and down into the dark yard, the words 'Leave him to me!' echoing in my ears. I went through the foggy streets until I found our house. The bells chimed two as I fought to find my key and get through the front door, but the door opened and there was my son in his nightgown.

'Mother!' he cried, 'Where have you been?'

I couldn't answer as the hall swam in front of my eyes and the darkness took me.

I awoke later to find myself tucked up in my bed. All my old symptoms that I had fought so hard to contain over the years had come back and I wondered if I would live long enough to see the light of Christmas Day. I listened out to see if the bells would tell me how long I had been asleep but all was silent as the room began to turn like a slow carousel making me feel terribly sick. Then, out of the swirling ceiling, came another apparition. Not the ghastly boiled lobster of a face that had belonged to Marley but a gentle giant whose eyes twinkled with merriment. In his hand he held a torch.

'Have you come to take me to my maker?' I whispered.

The ghost shook his head and, smiling with joy, proceeded to pour some incense from his torch. It came down upon me like a gentle rain from heaven and, in that moment, I knew true happiness just before I fell into a deep, deep sleep.

'Mother, here's the doctor to see you.' It was my dear Fred's voice as he tried to rouse me. He sounded desperately worried and, as I struggled to awake from what must have been the most beautiful sleep of my life, I found myself coming out with: 'It's all right dear Fred. I feel fine, never better.'

I sat up in bed and saw the doctor standing beside Fred with the sunlight streaming through the window behind them. The doctor insisted on examining me and insisted on taking no fee as it was Christmas Day and insisted on shaking his head in amazement at my recovery and insisted on passing on the news that my brother, the meanest man in London, had gone mad and had started sending huge turkeys to poor families and was seen to be dancing round his rooms in his nightshirt shouting and whooping.

After the doctor had said his goodbyes, Fred came in with some

Scattered Chapters 51

breakfast for me and asked: 'Could this be true? Could uncle have changed so rapidly?'

I took a sip of tea and smiled. 'Well, look at me,' I said. 'I have never felt so well...'

'... and last night...'

'... I collapsed in your arms...'

'... and I thought you...'

'I thought I would never live to see Christmas Day!'

There was such celebration that day. Every moment was a delight. Every face was alight and no task was a task at all, but a joy to perform. Soon, we were ready for the dinner but Fred was sure that his uncle would never come.

'The news could be a false rumour,' he maintained. 'I don't want you to get your hopes up, mother. But you know how these stories fly round the city. Do you remember the one about the Archbishop standing on his head and singing the Hallelujah chorus and how it turned out to be a prank played by a group of choirboys?'

I laughed then, for I knew this was no false news. I knew that Eben, my dear Eben had been visited by a ghost and that the ghost had told me: 'Leave him to me.' And I would never forget the apparition that visited me in the night and poured pure happiness onto me. But I could never tell Fred that. I had recovered from one illness and I didn't want to be treated for another — an illness of the mind. 'Wait and see,' I said to myself as the dining hour neared.

There was a knock at the door, voices from the hall, and I could hear Sarah, our young servant, sounding surprised. The door handle to the dining room slowly turned. Fred was looking out of the window and his lovely wife was sitting in the corner, her feet on a footstool for she was soon due to give me my first grandchild.

'𝔉𝔯𝔢𝔡.' A voice come through the crack in the door.

Both husband and wife started at the sound.

'𝔚𝔥𝔶, 𝔟𝔩𝔢𝔰𝔰 𝔪𝔶 𝔰𝔬𝔲𝔩!' 𝔠𝔯𝔦𝔢𝔡 𝔉𝔯𝔢𝔡, '𝔚𝔥𝔬'𝔰 𝔱𝔥𝔞𝔱?'

'𝔍𝔱'𝔰 𝔍. 𝔜𝔬𝔲𝔯 𝔲𝔫𝔠𝔩𝔢 𝔖𝔠𝔯𝔬𝔬𝔤𝔢. 𝔍 𝔥𝔞𝔳𝔢 𝔠𝔬𝔪𝔢 𝔱𝔬 𝔡𝔦𝔫𝔫𝔢𝔯. 𝔚𝔦𝔩𝔩 𝔶𝔬𝔲 𝔩𝔢𝔱 𝔪𝔢 𝔦𝔫, 𝔉𝔯𝔢𝔡?'

I smiled then. I was sure that my brother and I shared a secret and perhaps we would share it with each other one day, but for now, he was back. My dear Eben, his face transformed into the smiles I once knew, the shackles of his dread friend avarice, broken, and into my arms he came. 'Welcome home dear brother!' I cried, 'Welcome home!' And I gently smiled to myself as I looked over his shoulder at the amazed faces of my dear family.

Note: (Dickens' original words are in '𝔒𝔩𝔡 𝔰𝔱𝔶𝔩𝔢 𝔦𝔱𝔞𝔩𝔦𝔠𝔰')

Danny O'Connor **The Work of Angels**

Mixed Media on Canvas
50 cm by 61 cm
Signed O'Connor (lower right)

The Work of Angels

Marge walked down the corridor humming a tune that she didn't know where it came from.

'Mr Jones is having breathing difficulties in room sixteen,' said Nurse Peter as he rushed past in the opposite direction.

'I'm on it,' said Marge. 'Nobody dies if I can help it.'

'Didn't say he was dying, just...' Nurse Peter's voice died out as he disappeared down the corridor.

Room sixteen had all four beds occupied with elderly gentlemen. It was worth a visit just for the laughs: four brave men fighting for life and they all had a joke up their sleeves.

'Now, Mr Jones,' said Marge, wheeling the oxygen to the side of his bed and pulling the curtain round. 'You know what I said about breathing, you just got to do it. Here...' She put the oxygen mask over his mouth and nose and felt his pulse.

'I told him,' Mr Brown's voice came from behind the curtain. 'You need to breathe properly, Ken, or not at all. You're putting me off me crossword.'

'Mr Brown,' said Marge in mock outrage. 'You shouldn't be doing a crossword, it's the middle of the night.'

'Night, day? It's all the same to me,' came the answer. 'The only way I can tell is by who's on duty.'

'Well that won't tell you, Mr Brown. We're on shifts, see. I don't always work nights.'

'And I had you down as the Angel of the Night,' came the rejoinder.

'Angel, yes. Night, not necessarily,' Marge replied. 'The best way to know which it is, is to take your sedative when we give it to you.'

'Too worried I won't wake up again,' said Mr Brown.

'Don't be silly. We'll wake you up with a nice cup of tea.'

'Milk, two sugars.'

'Honestly, Mr Brown, I thought you were sweet enough,' said Marge. 'Now let me concentrate on Mr Jones here.' She looked at her watch, looked at the oxygen dial, and muttered to herself, 'If this doesn't get better, we'll have to put you on a ventilator.'

'You didn't put Boris on a ventilator,' Mr Brown's voice came from behind the curtain.

'You've got very good hearing for someone your age,' Marge replied.

'They're about the only part of me that hasn't packed up, me ears,' said Mr Brown, with a chuckle.

'I'm sorry to hear that, Mr Brown. Now let me concentrate on Mr Jones...'

Marge checked the dial and her patient's pulse again while she could hear Mr Brown saying quietly to himself: 'Down is definitely x-ray so nine across must begin with an 'x'. Now let me see... Begins with an 'x' — hit me and I plink? What kind of clue is that? Begins... with... an... x...'

Silence.

Scattered Chapters

Except, that is, for all the machines, the aircon, the buzz of the low-level lighting and a sudden exhibition of hi-vibe snoring by Mr Smyth.

This place is never quiet, thought Marge to herself. *It's a miracle anyone sleeps at all!*

She checked Mr Jones again to make sure he was breathing more comfortably with the help of his oxygen mask. All well, all quiet.

Quiet? No sound from Mr Brown? Has a miracle occurred and he's gone to sleep? Marge wondered. She quietly drew the curtain round Mr Jones' bed back and looked over towards Mr Brown. He didn't look right. He was sitting there with his mouth open and his lips had gone purple.

'Mr Brown? Mr Brown?' Marge pulled the emergency button.

Someone's calling my name: 'Mr Brown? Mr Brown?' Their voice fades into the distance and I am in my flat, looking out of the window. It's a small flat — just one bedroom, a sitting room, a kitchen and a tiny bathroom. I can remember back to the fifties and seeing my first bathroom and thinking what a miracle it was!

Anyway, here I am, sitting and looking out of the window. The advantage of this place is that it has a great view from fifteen storeys up; the disadvantage is that if the lift doesn't work, there's a lot of stairs to climb.

But, as I said, I'm looking out of the window at the view across the city and I'm noticing smoke. Something makes me think of cladding and I remember with a shock the letter that came through my door demanding that I pay thousands of pounds to have it replaced. If Sylvie was still here I could at least have shared the worry with her, but she's passed on and left me to fend for myself. I try not to worry about the letter: there's nothing I can do, there's nothing they can do, I haven't got thousands of pounds So that's that! But it still gets to me and I feel on edge all the time. The only answer is to get back to that crossword puzzle.

I shut the outside world out and look at the clue: 'Nine across, begins with an 'x' hit me and I plink.' What sort of clue is that?

Plink?

Blink?

Hit?

Shit! The smoke's getting thicker outside. I'm worrying, but I refuse to worry. Shut it out! Do the crossword. Then it will all go away.

But the smoke doesn't go away — outside my window it's getting thicker.

Cladding.

Letter.

Panic.

Crossword.

Nine across.

Stuck!

Nowhere to go. I'm stuck in this flat with smoke outside and no Sylvie to help me. If I could just get the clue...

It's no good, I'll have to get out of my chair and look out of the window to see what's going on out there.

Smoke's billowing up from below. The fire must be a few storeys down and it must be my block that's on fire. I can hear sirens now — they're making an odd beep-beep sound like someone's pulled a panic button. I can see a fire engine draw up below my window and on its roof it has an odd contraption: I would expect it to be a ladder but it looks more like a series of broad metal steps that get thinner as they get towards the front of the vehicle. They start to raise this weird contraption and it's coming higher and higher, stretching up into the air and directly towards my window. There's a crash of splintering glass as the top step which is only one-foot-wide smashes straight through my window. I want to climb out onto the strange contraption but it doesn't look very safe and there's no fireman to give me a helping hand. The smoke comes billowing into my sitting room making it hard to breathe. I start to choke from the acrid fumes. I will die if I stay here. I will die if I climb out of the window and fall fifteen storeys. I can't get the clue and and I can't forget the letter.

'Somebody help me!' I scream, and like a miracle a face appears at the window. It's Marge, our nurse — The Angel of the Night.

'Come on,' she says as she reaches out to take my hand. 'Nobody dies if I can help it.'

I take her hand and she helps me onto the giant...

'Xylophone!' I gasp, getting the clue at last.

'That was a close shave,' Marge said as she sipped a cup of tea. 'Honestly, they're like four budgies in there. I turn my back for one minute and one of them falls off his perch!'

'So what was it he said when you brought him round?' asked Nurse Peter.

'Xylophone!'

'Xylo-what?'

'Xylophone — it was the clue he was trying to get when he passed out. That crossword nearly killed him. Anyway,' said Marge finishing her tea, 'I'd better get back before something else happens.'

A couple of days later, Marge walked down the corridor humming a tune that she couldn't remember where it came from. It niggled her that she couldn't place it. There was a name attached to it, an unusual name.

'Hullo, gentlemen,' she said cheerily as she entered the room. 'How are we this morning?'

'Not so much of the gentlemen,' replied Mr Brown with mock grumpiness. 'We're a bunch of old men here, waiting to meet our maker.'

'Not if I can help it,' said Marge.

'I'm not waiting to meet my maker,' piped up Mr Smyth from the other side of the room. '*I'm* waiting to meet my daughter Rachel.'

'Taking you home is she?' Mr brown asked.

'That's it.'

'Thank God for that,' said Mr Brown. 'No more of your snoring to keep us awake at night.'

'It's not the snoring that keeps you awake, Mr Brown, it's your blessed crosswords. And how are you, Mr Jones?' Marge said, changing the subject.

Scattered Chapters   57

'Breathing better now?'

'Yes thank you,' came the quiet reply.

'Speaking of crosswords,' Mr Brown interrupted. 'I'm really stuck on this one. It's a bloody music one again. Two words down six letters and seven letters both beginning with a G — great guitarist.'

'Well that's it,' said Mr Smyth. 'Obvious. They've just told you the answer — Great Guitarist.'

'No, no, no, they'd never do that and anyway it obviously doesn't fit,' replied Mr Brown, scornfully.

'No George, don't do that!' Marge interrupted, suddenly. 'Mr Green, please leave your catheter alone!'

'George!' Mr Brown joined in. 'Don't play with yourself, it's dirty.'

She heard a peal of laughter from next door and it brought to mind a man she'd seen only yesterday who was in with pneumonia. Long curly hair, lots of smiles, long fingernails on his right hand.

'Gordon Giltrap,' she said out loud.

'It works,' said Mr Brown after a pause. 'How did you know?'

'Aha...' said Marge, realising that she should be discreet.

'He wrote 'Heartsong' didn't he,' Mr Jones joined in quietly from his corner.

That's it. Thought Marge to herself, *That's what I keep humming.* 'Heartsong!'

Detail

Scattered Chapters 59

Carl Knibb **The Stars Look Down on Linda**

Acrylic on Canvas
51 cm by 41 cm
Signed Carl Knibb (lower right)

The Stars Look Down on Linda

'*Two, it takes two,*' Matti thought as he walked through the shopping centre. He was part of a two once, only it was really a one-and-a-half. He was one and she was a half — half because she was actually in love with someone else!

A shopping centre is not a place where you might expect the magic of love to happen — Matti may wish for it as hard as he liked, but then Matti knew that his fairy godmother was unlikely to appear with a magic wand and find him his princess. Shopping centres are created to sell things. '*Can't buy me love,*' Matti thought to himself, '*But I could buy all sorts of things for my love... if I had a love.*'

A large teddy bear with a pink bow tie seemed to glare out of a shop window at him as he passed: '*You going to buy me, or what? She'd love me, you know. She would!*'

But she wouldn't because there wasn't a she.

'*What am I doing wandering around this shopping centre, anyway?*' Matti asked himself. '*It's not Christmas. No upcoming birthdays, that is,*' and here he felt a jolt of guilt, '*unless I've forgotten someone.*'

He was so caught up in trying to remember if he'd forgotten someone that he tripped on something that was sticking out of a doorway.

'Sorry,' he said automatically as he staggered across the pavement, colliding with a young lady carrying a load of shopping bags. She dropped her bags with a 'Bloody Hell!' and looked at him. 'Why can't you look where you're going?' she yelled at him.

'Sorry,' said Matti as he stooped down to help her with the bags. 'Let me...'

Was this an opportunity? Had his fairy godmother struck out with her wand after all?

'No! Keep away from me! You've done enough damage already!' shouted the young lady, glaring at him as she picked up her bags.

Matti guessed that this wasn't his opportunity. Pretty though she was, he had the feeling that she wouldn't be the warm companion he was looking for, and anyway, before he had a chance to think of anything else to say, she was strutting off on her high heels, her bags gathered up, without a backward glance.

He stood there for a moment, his eyes smarting, the general public ignoring him and his embarrassment.

'Sorry,' came a girl's voice from behind him, and he looked round.

There in a doorway was what looked like a bundle of clothes and the voice came from the bundle. As he looked he could see a foot that had

Scattered Chapters   61

been extended out onto the pavement being withdrawn into the bundle.

'No, I should look where I'm going,' he said. Always the gallant one, Matti. He looked down into the doorway and spotted a polystyrene cup with a a few coins in it. It was at that moment that something peculiar happened to his mind — a different way of seeing things. He tended to avoid conversation or even any contact with people who lived on the streets — the closest he got was buying a copy of Big Issue from time to time. He had little money to spare himself, and had been brought up to be suspicious of those who didn't work. But now, as he looked down at this girl sheltering in a doorway covered in a heap of clothes to keep her warm, he just couldn't walk away.

'Hey,' said Matti. 'Would you like a cup of coffee?'

The bundle stirred, a small triangular face appeared appeared and was caught by the light.

'Why?' she said. She sounded suspicious.

'Well... I... er... thought it's a bit cold, and er... you might like to come into a café and get warm.'

'No strings attached?'

'Strings? What do you mean? Strings?' It might be worth mentioning, at this point, that Matti was of Polish origin and didn't know all the colloquial British expressions.

'You don't want anything.' The girl spoke more clearly, now.

'Just to give you a cup of coffee and get you in the warm.' Matti was beginning to feel that he'd made a mistake and should walk away from this unwise encounter.

'Okay.' She started to get up off the pavement.

'Too late,' thought Matti as he reached out a hand to help her up. His hand was declined and the girl quickly stuffed her belongings into two tatty jute shopping bags.

'I'm Matti,' he said, the alarm bells ringing inside his head, saying *'Don't tell her your name!'*

'Gwen,' said Gwen as she tottered along beside him, stiff from her sleep on the pavement.

Matti looked down at Gwen — Gwen looked up at Matti.

'Shall we go in here?' Matti indicated a Wetherspoons that looked nice and spacious, he didn't want to be too close to other people while he tried this foolish experiment in 'helping the poor'.

They sat by the window and Matti ordered coffee for two and a cheese toastie for Gwen. He stood by the counter and looked at her. She was very small, young, but he couldn't determine her age — he guessed at twenties. He'd noticed that she had a very clear way of speaking with a slight accent that he couldn't place.

The tray of coffees and cheese toastie in his hand, he returned to their table.

'Thanks,' said Gwen.

'That's okay,' said Matti. *'What now, do I ask how she came to be on the streets?'*

'So what do you do, Matti?' Gwen took the initiative.

'Oh, I collect the recycling bins,' he said, and for the first time he felt proud of his job. 'That's in the mornings, and then I do decorating work when I can get it.'

'Decorating? Painting a house you mean?' said Gwen. 'I'd like a house.' She stopped abruptly and took shelter behind her cheese toastie.

'I live in a flat,' Matti said. Somehow that felt better than comparing her non-house-ness to an actual house. 'It's very small,' he went on, warming to this angle. 'Just a kitchen-diner, bedroom and bathroom. It's over a sweet shop.' Why was he telling her this?

'I used to have a house,' Gwen said, putting her toastie-shield down. 'It was lovely. A garden. A hot-tub. All mod cons. But I lost it.'

'Lost it?' *How can you lose a house?* Matti wondered.

'Easily,' said Gwen, reading his thoughts. 'You can lose a house easily. You get a mortgage because you've got a good job. You rely on the money from that job and it gets better and better with more and more money. You take on more debt so that you can have the things you want — now! And then… you fall into bad habits — gambling was mine — and you fall right off the end! They don't want you anymore, you're screwed, you have minus money, and before you know it, you've lost your house and you're on the streets.'

'But… but that's terrible,' said Matti, aghast.

'Happens,' said Gwen tucking into her cheese toastie again. 'Anyway, it's not as bad as what happened to my great-grandfather.'

'What?'

'My great-grandfather was a miner in the Rhonda valley before the First World War. There was a miner's strike and Churchill, Churchill mind you, set the army on them. My great-grandfather starved to death.'

'My grandfather was killed in Wujek.' Matti came out with this before he could stop himself. 'He was pro-Solidarity and fifteen of the miners were shot dead by Polish forces.'

'So he was a miner too?' said Gwen, wiping her lips carefully with her napkin. 'And you're Polish.'

'Yes,' said Matti. 'Does that matter? You're Welsh.'

Gwen reached her hand out across the table and Matti, for some reason that had nothing to do with what he was thinking, put his hand out… and they shook hands.

'So tell me,' Matti said as he laid down another tray — this time with coffee with chocolate muffins. 'About your job, and how you got there. Mine is very simple. Left school. Learnt the decorating trade from my uncle and landed a job working for the council collecting recycling bins. Cold in the morning, but I love it. Simple.' *Why am I opening up like this?* He asked himself. *I never open up like this.*

'Mine's a long story,' Gwen replied. She'd been to the toilets and cleaned herself up a little. Matti thought she looked… more… was it grownup? Together? To be reckoned with? Anyway, she was more visible, somehow.

'When I was at school I used to sing a lot. They said I had a good voice, my parents and the school, so I went in for the Eisteddfod every year.'

'Eisteddfod?' Matti tried to pronounce it. 'What's that?'

'Oh, it's a Welsh thing — a mixture of a competition and a festival. They're very big in Wales. Anyway, one year I won the singing in the National Eisteddfod it and was offered a scholarship to the LCM.'

'LCM?'

'Sorry, London College of Music.'

'Sounds... er... very grand.' Matti was impressed.

'It was. I had a great time there and really enjoyed getting to know the other students and taking part in musical events. But when I left, it was really difficult to get work as a singer and I saw an advert for a job in advertising.' Gwen laughed at her unintended joke. 'At that time, a lot of firms were looking for music graduates as they thought musicians would have creative minds and could see outside the box. Anyway, I got the job and started working in advertising. It was really fast moving, loads of pressure and loads of money. They found that I had a knack for good slogans and a talent in copywriting, so soon I was high-flying and earning a fortune. I bought a house, got a boyfriend who had expensive tastes. Borrowed lots of money. Lived the high life — a whole lifetime away from my poor background in South Wales. I never went to see them, my family. Never gave them a penny, though they were struggling. I was so caught up in the glam, fake world of advertising that I believed in it. Somebody said: 'Don't believe your own publicity'. Too true!'

Gwen looked down at her muffin and shook her head.

Matti wanted to reach out and hold her hand but didn't.

'Then it all went wrong. My boyfriend deserted me for someone with more money, but kept the sports car I bought him.'

Matti gasped.

'I got depressed, started using coke — there was plenty around — and got into gambling. My work suffered and they employed someone else better, cheaper and younger and suddenly I had no job, a massive gambling debt, a coke habit. My lovely house which I'd taken out a large mortgage to buy was repossessed by the bank and I was on the streets — literally.'

Matti was aghast: 'How long have you been living like this?'

'A couple of years. To start off with I was on the coke, that was until I realised the only way to feed my habit was by being a sex worker, so I managed to get off it.' She shivered.

'What about your family?'

'I can't go back there! I simply can't. They'd say 'I told you so', and things like, 'how could you waste your talent?''

Matti, who liked the Prodigal Son story, wondered if she was right about that. 'So how do you live?'

'Begging, mainly. Get enough for a night in a hostel, then see what the next day brings. Living in the moment!' She laughed.

'Doesn't sound great to me,' Matti said.

'It's not,' said Gwen.

'Couldn't you do something to make a living?' Matti's upbringing overtook his reticence in asking this question.

'Like what? Work in a bank?' Gwen's eyes blazed.

'Wait, there's a magazine. Here, I've got one here.' Matti reached into his jacket pocket and picked out a folded publication he'd bought just outside the shopping centre. Strangely, he couldn't even visualise the person he'd bought it from.

'What? The Big Issue? I wouldn't be seen dead selling that rag. People would think I was a street person...'

'But you are...' Matti couldn't bring himself to say 'a street person.'

'And anyway, it's full of crap.'

'No it's not. Just have a look — really interesting articles, reviews, news.'

Gwen was beginning to get up from her chair, but Matti put his hand gently on her arm and opened the magazine so that she could read it.

'Oh,' was all she said and sat down again. After all, there was half a mug of coffee to drink and an unfinished muffin on the table.

Matti looked at his watch. 'Whoops, got to go. I said I'd help an elderly lady with her shopping.' He got up and left Gwen who was already engrossed in an article about a music festival.

He looked back. He'd felt something. It hadn't occurred to him that she might ever be... no that was impossible, but still she was the most interesting... no, more than that, girl he'd ever met.

It was months before Matti saw Gwen again. It was a warm afternoon and he was walking down to a square in the middle of a neighbouring town where he'd just started doing up a house. It was for the elderly lady that he helped, and she had said that he could live in it at a low rent when it was liveable-in. The house was a wreck. But hey, what an opportunity! His clothes were covered in paint and plaster and he was taking a break before having a last go at 'updating' the bathroom.

As he neared the square, he heard a woman's voice singing. It sounded like classical music, something from an opera, maybe? Yes, Puccini, he was sure it was — his parents liked Puccini, they were always playing it. He was struck how well it sounded without an orchestra, so plaintive, such beautiful melody. And the singer, though she had a rough edge to her voice, knew how to deliver it.

He rounded the corner into the square, and there she was, Gwen! selling The Big Issue! standing in the middle of the square. A big voice for such a small woman. But people were ignoring her, he couldn't believe it, just walking past as though she didn't exist. Plugged into their personal hi-fi, or phones. And here was this glorious music. *We're ants,* Matti thought.

He stood and listened for a while until the aria came to an end and then plucked up the courage to go and speak to her.

'Hello,' Matti said.

'Big Issue!' Gwen said, and then looked up and saw him. 'Hey it's you...'

'Matti,' he finished for her. 'I see you're selling...'

'Big Issue!' Gwen shouted at a passing shopper. 'Yes, and it was you who got me onto it.'

Matti swelled with pride, but at the same time he felt strangely shy. This young woman was no longer a bundle of rags to be rescued from a shop doorway. She was herself: proud, talented, standing there and trying to sell the...

'Big Issue!' Gwen shouted.

Matti overcame his shyness and said, 'Would you like to meet on the church green after you've finished. We could have coffee.'

She looked at him in his dirty work-clothes and laughed. 'Okay, seven-thirty, by the memorial.'

He walked away, his heart strangely full, and listened as she started singing something else classical that he couldn't place. *'What a transformation!'* he thought as he walked out of earshot. It was only then that he realised that he hadn't even bought a Big Issue off her.

She was sitting on the grass by the memorial as Matti walked over, carrying a tray of coffees and chocolate muffins.

'You've scrubbed up well,' she laughed.

'So have you, I mean...' Matti stumbled to a halt.

'The Oxfam shop's great for clothes,' Gwen laughed.

'So... er... how's it been, I mean how...?'

'I took your advice and tracked down the Big Issue Foundation and started selling a few months ago.'

'Do you always sing? Nobody seems to take any notice.'

'But the butcher opposite likes it, so I sing for him. I don't think it sells any more Big Issues but, hey, I enjoy it... finding that again... and look,' Gwen thrust a Big Issue at him, 'I've got an article in there. Told them I use to write copy for advertising, and bingo! they asked me for a contribution. Page five, look...'

It was an article about a book by A J Cronin — The Stars Look Down.

'That's the strike during which my great-grandfather died of starvation,' Gwen continued. 'The book tells it all really well and it seems so significant now with the increase in poverty and food banks in this country.'

'But things are better now than back then, aren't they?'

'I don't know.' Gwen lay back on the grass and looked up into the early evening sky. The sun was already glowing red and the stars were just beginning to become visible.

Matti lay back too. *'The stars look down on... Gwen and Matti,'* he thought, but he said: 'I'm doing up a house and I am going to live in it.'

'Oh, a house.' Gwen sat up. 'I've dreamed of living in a house again.'

Then Matti said, without knowing why, 'Would you like to come and live in it when it's ready?' Then he immediately regretted it.

Gwen sipped her coffee and took a bite out of her chocolate muffin. She chewed it slowly with a look of fierce concentration, as though testing the flavour of his question, then swallowed.

'I might,' she said.

Gary O'Neil **The Wounded Healer**

Acrylic on Canvas
61 cm by 77 cm
Signed Gary O'Neil (lower left)

The Wounded Healer

Everyone is on their mobile phones, looking at each other and talking into their screens, but I cannot touch them, heal them, feel their warm vibration of life going into my hands. I can talk into a screen too, but so much is missing. If I am with you in space I can give, I can change what is harming you, but take away my touch and almost all is lost. I am like a tiny feather on your skin, almost undetectable, possibly irritating, rather than the fullblown body-ness of my true care.

There are some who can cure from miles away — their voice, their wisdom, changing minds and souls. But mine is a pithy experience, an on-body experience, not an on-line experience.

Isolation is an intense experience for me. The wounds that I have and the wounds that I have taken away from others grow larger in my mind. No escape for the sadness, no escape for the hurt, no remedy for the pain and suffering that I find in all mankind. Think of me and maybe, just maybe, that thought will reach me, not online, not through touch but through the free air and sun and moisture that surrounds us all.

I drove to the hills and I took a walk along the Ridgeway — an ancient path that follows high contours from east to west. Up there I felt the wind of grace, the timeless pace of feet once trodden before me. I saw a figure coming towards me from a distance. As it came closer I could see that it was an old man with a stick. His face was creased with smiles and his piercing eyes roamed this way and that, taking in the details of his surroundings as he moved along the path towards me. Then he saw me and I felt a thrill pass through my body. His face was a light palace filled with wisdom. 'He can heal me,' I thought. 'He knows.' And as he neared me, I could feel the warmth from his body, almost as if he was touching me. A thing he couldn't do, mustn't do. Although he was six feet away from me when he passed by, acknowledging my presence with a smile and a 'hello', I felt a charge pass between us and in that moment I heard a music that was both gentle and firm; expansive but containing; and it held me, held me as I walked on not daring to look back in case I had simply imagined him. The sound of that music expanded and developed inside me, taking in the rolling hills and valleys and bringing to mind a broader place — a place where the sweep of lakes and mountains was too big to fathom. And I felt as though I would burst with the it-ness of it, the there-ness of being there but not being able to contain it in my hands and mind — just allowing it to be and resting in its gigantic healing power.

I have just come home and everything's changed. I am alone. I am wounded. I hurt. I carry all this pain. I am damaged. There are things wrong with me. So wrong, it seems, that I could never help anyone else, let alone heal them.

But now I can see something else, and I see it clearly. I can heal because I suffer and in my suffering I can be with the damaged one as a sister so that we can suffer together and find a path to health holding each other's hands. I cannot, I will not, stand back and be the expert — writing reports, looking at you from the outside. I will not be learned and full of advice that you will never remember. I will hobble along next to you and we'll find our way together up the mountain to the place where we can see more, and feel more and find healing in the expanse laid out before us.

I sit down at my table with a mug of steaming tea and smell its warm fragrance, and as I do so, the music that I heard as the old man passed me, comes back in full force. That tune, that grandeur, that fullness of life will remain with me and hold me so that I can truly be The Wounded Healer.

Detail

Sonja Burliston **Turning Earth**
Silk Screen Print
50 cm by 38,5 cm

Turning Earth

I see the gleaming prongs of the fork coming down towards me, the sun, which dazzles me, caught in glints on the clean metal. Closer it comes as I prepare to receive it. The fork, my nemesis, my changer, my turner. Would you leave me alone to harden and get populated by rough weeds or would you turn me to rescue me and bring my damp goodness up to the air? I'm always afraid of the pain at this point, but actually it's more like being scratched and massaged. A dizzy feeling too, as I turn upside down. But it makes me laugh when I rest there, exposed and waiting.

There's a pause then, and I take the time to reflect on what you have done in past years. For it is each year that this happens. I know, because I counted each time my great mother earth turned and it was three hundred and sixty-five times. Last year, I remember bulbs. They were silky smooth as you thrust them just under my surface. Like globes from the Christmas tree that I see every year in your window. The bulbs rested for a time and didn't speak to me. And while they slept I received frost, my cold friend who breaks up my surface and kills off the itchy things for a while. Then, with a slow rustling sound, a small root came out of one bulb, then another and another until there were roots everywhere. And they spoke and cackled to each other in their thin voices. There was a thrusting movement in both directions — shoots growing out of the top of the bulb as the roots thrust downwards. The shoots seemed almost desperate for the light. Fearing they would drown in my earth, they squirmed upwards to feel the release as they reached the surface — the sun warm on their ends. But not satisfied with that, they grew ever higher, parts branching out into long green leaves and each central stem carrying its precious load of furled flower up, up as far as it could reach. To see the yellow trumpet high in the sun and to feel the the nutrients and moisture being taken from me to do this was a joy, a creativity, a still dance.

'I shifted my axis this year,' my mother earth told me. 'Every now and then, since Mars decided to collide with me, I have changed my view of the great sun. It's a natural thing caused by planets and other forces around me, and to be honest, it makes me feel better. I don't think the people on my surface notice, except... there might be the odd person who noticed the sun going down in a slightly different place. You'd have to look carefully, notice. But this year I have shifted my axis a bit and my children may notice a slight change in the seasons. Mind you, the people that are on my surface at the moment have done so many things to their atmosphere that it could be hard to notice that subtle difference. Like the dinosaurs before them, they will come and they will go, these people. I'm sad because, in spite of their destructiveness, they are very interesting creatures. But I will carry on as I have done for billions of years. Perhaps some of my less

recent occupants, like wood lice and nematodes, will stay on to keep my children company.'

Ah, she's back, the gardener who just turned me over, and in her hands she has something that I can't quite see. That's the trouble with being earth, one's point of view from the surface is only upwards. True, I can see down and feel down into my soil with such detail, such fulfilling enjoyment. For some earth that is not so true as they are perpetually squashed by heavy machinery or they can't see upwards because they're imprisoned beneath tar and concrete. But for me, the garden earth, there is at least a chance of enjoying what's above me.

Oh, here it comes. She going to make a hole and put a new occupant in it. Company for the winter. The bulb is small and almost round. It has a funny hairy topknot — I dare say that will disappear over time. Another hole and another bulb, then another and another. They are all slightly different but they have their silky smooth but slightly peeling coats to keep them safe asleep before they have to do their work in the spring. That is, unless my friend the squirrel digs them up and eats them. He's my friend because he brings me all sorts of stories and interesting nuts and then forgets where he put them so that they grow, unexpected by the gardener, but welcomed by me.

Now what are these bulbs? Hmm... I'm hearing a small creaky voice. 'Crrrrocusss', it says. 'Crrrrrocusss.'

Welcome crocus!

Detail

Chloe Doyle **Precious**
Pencil Watercolour and Ink on paper
30 cm by 21 cm
Signed C. Doyle (lower left)

Precious

By Hilary Giltrap

Precious as rock to the stone.

Precious as blood to the bone.

Precious the earth to the tree

Precious your love is to me.

Precious the pearl to the shell.

Precious the bronze to the bell.

Precious the sky to the star.

Precious the map to afar.

Precious the days of my life.

Precious as I am your wife.

Eternal the earth and the sky,

The sun, moon, stars...

YOU and I.

Sue Martin **The Melody Weaver's Son**
Watercolour on Paper
23 cm by 35 cm

The Melody Weaver's Son

Where to begin? For this story is as old as time — as new as the scent of fresh-cut grass. It has no beginning and it has no end. But we could start with a place.

The Melody Weaver lived in a small cottage on the edge of the great forest of the north. The cottage had changed shape over time: first it was wooden, then mud and wood, then Yak-hide for a while. None of these buildings lasted long, as you can imagine, but one day a very clever builder from a country where buildings had to be solid enough to resist regular earthquakes, built the Melody Weaver of that time a house of stone. It was so well-crafted that you could hardly see the join between one stone and another. And the stones were so big and so strong that it seemed that they could last for ever. In later times successive Melody Weavers had built on extra parts to give themselves more room but they never lasted long. Some natural event, whether flood, storm, or earthquake, would reduce them to so much rubble, leaving the original stone building intact — the magic of those perfect joints and well-chosen stones out-lasting any later attempt to make the building grander or more complex.

So now you can see why this Melody Weaver lived in a *small* cottage on the edge of the great forest of the north. And anyway, the melodies flowed in his mind so much that he had no thoughts of building an extra bathroom or a grand entrance hall or a west wing to his house. He had no time for that and he chose to live a simple life with his wife and child and weave his melodies for those who needed them, so that they could hum them or put their own words to them as they worked in fields or castles, citadels or ports, all over the known world.

I said the cottage was small, and it was. It had a main room that you could swing a cat in (but being the gentle man that he was, he would never do such a cruel thing as swing a cat or any other animal for that matter) and at one end was a large fire for heating and cooking that had a large beaten sheet of brass attached to the wall at the back that projected the heat out into the room. Above the fire, the roof had a small opening to let the smoke out and on particularly productive days the tunes of the Melody Weaver would join the smoke going out of the roof and make strange and beautiful shapes that could be seen from miles around. Some said that the birds picked up these melodies and that's why the blackbirds,

Scattered Chapters   79

thrushes and robins that lived in the woods nearby were such good singers. Behind the big fire was a separate smaller room where the water came up from a spring in the ground. It was used for drinking and washing — the little room acted as a bathroom-come-scullery. Above this room was a loft where the family could sleep and it was reached by a ladder from the floor below.

That's about it... oh but I forgot to say there was a little brook that ran in front of the house, with a kitchen garden leading down to it that provided all their vegetables.

⫿⫿

As I said, the Melody Weaver had a wife and a child. Just one child, mind, and that child was a son, his son. And as his son grew, he became more and more different from his father. Whereas the Melody Weaver accepted life as it was, his son had a restless mind and was always asking questions. When his father explained how the craft of melody weaving was passed from father to son and always had been, the boy asked:

'Always? Have Melody Weavers always had sons to pass their craft on to? And what about the daughters? Can they be melody weavers? And what happens if there are no children at all?'

His father pursed his lips and was silent. He didn't want to think about those times when it didn't all go according to the God-given plan.

'Well, there have been times,' he answered, thinking back over the stories that he had heard. 'Times when daughters have become melody weavers, and very good ones too, or so I have heard.'

'But what if there are no children at all?'

'If that happens, then a child that is found to have the *gift*, is brought to this house and leaves his family to learn from the Melody Weaver.'

'Isn't that rather cruel?' the boy asked. 'Taking a child from his loved ones, from his family, just so that the melody weaving can carry on?'

'Yes,' said his father, his own thoughts having been reflected by the boy's question. 'It is hard for that boy, but... the tradition must go on. Melody must not be allowed to die out.'

'But what about if a child who is born to it, doesn't want to be the next Melody Weaver?'

'Don't you want to be one? Is that what you're saying?' his father asked, suddenly worried. 'It's a wonderful thing to be the maker, the weaver of melodies. The best job in the world.'

'But supposing the child doesn't have the talent for making tunes?' the boy asked, frowning.

'But you do,' said his father, earnestly. 'I've heard you singing and I know you have the gift. You *do* want to take over from me don't you?'

'I don't know,' the boy answered disconsolately, and walked away down to the brook leaving his father to ponder and worry about what all this meant.

As he watched his son grow, the Melody Weaver felt an increasing sense of foreboding. He could see that his boy was growing to be less and less like him. Whereas the weaver was quite short and sturdily built, his son was tall and thin.

'*He takes after his mother,*' the weaver thought. '*She's thin and a bit taller than me. But I worry about her too sometimes. She's so frail.*'

And so she was. There was something around the eyes as though the skin was made of the thinnest paper and her grey eyes shone almost too much, as if they were seeing beyond to another world.

'*Don't leave me,*' he thought, though he never said it to her. '*Please don't leave me, I love you so much and I can't bring our son up on my own.*'

His son also had those eyes, although they were keener, more intent, as though he was trying to see past the hills and trees that surrounded their little cottage.

▯▯▯

Then, one day, she was gone. She didn't die in bed. There were no last-minute partings, no holding her hand as her soul passed to another realm, no chance to wish her good luck on her journey.

She walked slowly towards the forest that grew behind their cottage. He watched her as the shafts of early morning sunlight lit up her long silver hair, her right shoulder and hip. Then gradually as the light hit her, it started to go through her. She became misty, transparent, as she neared the wall of dark trees. Then she was just a wisp of smoke, then just a memory.

'*Just a memory,*' the Melody Weaver thought, as he wrote his saddest tune. A tune that spread gently through the known world giving comfort to those who had lost loved ones. A truly great tune that people could put their own words to, sing at wakes and funerals, sing to remind themselves of the love of those gone before them. It was, in fact, his greatest melody, a melody inhabited by his Elena whom he had lost but who had come back to him forever through the medium of this piece of music.

During this time, he hardly exchanged any words with his son. They went on through their lives together, cooking and eating together, looking and walking together. They searched the forest for signs of Elena. They listened to the birds that sang strange rich songs and wondered if she was one of them. They stood still as huge bears passed them. They found magical clearings where ghostly dances could be seen — figures that floated, unclear in the mist and sunlight. But they never saw her.

They were silent, but they were together. And, oddly, the Melody Weaver felt closer to his son at this time. His son would often sit beside him as he weaved his melodies. Sometimes he would catch a phrase from his father and continue it in a new and unexpected direction. The music became their conversation and the Melody Weaver had high hopes that his son would become better than him in his craft. He certainly had the skill and he worked so hard to improve his music. Instead of looking out to the world, his son looked to his father and took comfort from the walls of the ancient cottage that they shared their lives in.

Finally, they broke their silence. The father began to talk of how he met his Elena at a dance in the village that lay across the brook, down the hill, through the trees. They had danced all night, he remembered, it was midsummer solstice and the whole village stayed awake through the revels. Elena's parents were pleased that their only daughter should be married to the Melody Weaver and had great hopes of enjoying grandchildren from such a union.

When he was born, the Melody Weaver told his son, his grandparents came to see him. They held him proudly in their arms and talked of other solstices when this little child would dance with them all. Sadly, this never came to pass as Elena's parents had to move away to find work, and visits became increasingly rare as age and distance made it difficult for them to manage the journey to the forests of the north. Then they lost all contact with them, the weaver told his son. It was what happened in the world now, families were split up by the new growing economies. Old rural communities were decaying and the cities of the south were growing.

'I should like to see the cities of the south, one day,' the son told his father.

'There's not much there,' his father said. 'Just a lot of noise. You're better off here.'

Years went by, and father and son became closer. The Melody Weaver saw his boy grow into a young man, he heard his son become ever more talented and ingenious at weaving melodies of his own, and he knew that one day his brilliant son would surpass him in music.

But, and there's always a but, he also knew that his son needed a wife. He saw how he looked with his keen eyes over the rolling hills and woods to the south, and how he longed to leave home and find his true love. And he remembered the words from *The Prophet:* [1]

"Your children are not your children. They are the sons and daughters of Life's longing for itself… For life goes not backward nor tarries with yesterday. You are the bows from which your children as living arrows are sent forth."

And so he started sending out word to see if anyone could find his son a wife. But the population was sparse in that part of the world and most young adults of suitable age had left to find work in the cities of the south. Those that remained were already betrothed or married and all other adults were their parents' age or older still. The nearest village, where the Melody Weaver had met his Elena was virtually a ghost town now with just a couple of aged brothers eking out a sparse living from the land and living in a broken-down old farmhouse.

After much discussion and head scratching the father and son decided

---

1. Quotation from The Prophet by Kahlil Gilbran.

to look north, to go into the great northern forest and see if there were people that lived there. Surely there might be settlements of people living in the north, beyond the great barrier of trees. True, there had never been signs of living people coming from there — only the spirits that they had witnessed all those years ago when they searched fruitlessly for Elena. The Melody Weaver was in favour of this idea because it took them in the opposite direction from the noisy cities of the south, and his son went along with it, partly because he hoped he would find signs of his mother, whom he so missed in his heart of hearts.

They got enough provisions together for a few days walking out and a few days returning and set out one spring morning with high hopes. They were together on this adventure, father and son, a solid unbeatable pair of rugged musicians carrying their magic melody weaving with them.

They used a compass and fixed on a trail that went north. There was

Detail

no actual path, but to start with they were able to cut a fairly straight course north through oak and ash, rowan and birch. When they came to the firs that grew closer together, the going became harder, only easing off when they came to the spiritfilled glades. The silence in these parts was oppressive, so father and son took it in turns to come up with suitable walking melodies that filled the forest around them with a light beauty that melted the cold shadows of the silent firs.

On the third day they came to a part of the forest where the trees grew taller and more sparsely. The cold wind blew through this land of giant redwoods and they could see snow capped mountains ahead of them. They had not come prepared for such cold weather and their singing stopped as they started to shiver and slide over the icy ground. All that could be heard now was the howl of the wind — this land was dead, they thought, and they looked at each other as they stumbled to a halt. No one could live here — the only thing to do was to return. This search had left them nowhere.

Then they heard the singing. It was a pure, high woman's voice and it called to them. They had to find the source of this beautiful sound which reached mysteriously deep into their souls. They knew it, and although they had never heard it before, they had heard something like it — Elena singing her son to sleep. The singing led them on up into the mountains. The trees were sparse and stunted now and the wind pushed them up the slopes until they came to a cave.

They could hear that the singing came from the cave and could see a light flickering from somewhere in the darkness. Glad of the shelter they trod carefully on the bare stone floor. The singing got louder as they neared the light which they could now see was a fire lit right at the back of the cave. A woman with silvery hair was sitting facing the fire and as they drew near, she stopped and all that they could hear was the drone of the wind outside and the sound of the crackling fire.

'Elena?' the Melody Weaver whispered.

'Yes,' came the answer. 'I am your Elena and I will always be yours. You have come at last. I have waited so long. I know what has driven you here. Our son needs a wife. She must have a child so that your melody weaving can be passed on. But it is not as you think — great change is coming to our world. North must meet south, east must meet west and a new wind of creation must blow in our world.'

'Elena,' the Melody Weaver was on his knees a few feet behind her. 'Please turn round so that I can embrace you. I have loved you and missed you for so long...' He couldn't go on, and his son stood behind him, looking at his mother's back, the tears streaming down his face.

'If I turn round,' Elena replied, gently, 'you will see me for a moment and then I will be gone and you will never see me again in this world. If that is what you want, then I shall do so, for I long to join the world of the spirits now and be in a place where I can see you and watch over you. But first, I must tell you this: our son must journey to the south to find his true love. She will not be what he expects but he will know when he meets her. It will be a long journey and he will discover many things and peoples that he never knew existed. But he must do this: north must meet south, east must meet west.'

Then she turned and they saw her beautiful face aged into creases of love and care. The Melody Weaver reached out to her and her son rushed forwards so that they could all hold each other in an embrace. For a moment they were all together. The two men could feel her slight body in their arms, and then she slipped away and vanished, leaving the feeling of her warm body behind.

Without a word, the two men left the cave, their arms round each other as they descended the mountainside and into the woods. It was a hard journey back and they hardly said a word to each other. No melody left their lips. Only the sound of the wind and the rustle of the trees accompanied their journey home. Once, they passed through a glade where misty shapes danced and they looked and looked to see if they could see Elena, but they couldn't be sure. That wisp of hair might have been hers, those trailing fingers, the small bare foot. The dance stopped and they tore themselves away and passed through the forest without further incident until they got to their old cottage.

It was a sunny day, some weeks later, when the son parted from his father to take the long arduous journey to the south. They had prepared themselves for this moment and the Melody Weaver had passed onto his son all the skills and gifts that he could give. They had discussed Elena and what she had meant, but had come to no conclusion other than the son must take his father's compass and set it on south, and to the south he must go.

The Melody Weaver stood by the brook and hugged his son and then watched him step over it and down the path that would take him out into the world. As he watched, he realised how much he had become immersed in his task to produce melodies for the world but how little he knew about it. His heart was divided — he was terribly sad to see his son go away from him, never knowing when he would see him again, but he was joyful at the same time, knowing that he and Elena had drawn back their bow and released the arrow that was their son, to go which ever way it would. And he could feel the freedom surge through his veins!

Days went by, then weeks, then months as the Melody Weaver struggled to create even one tune. No news of his son came to him and the few tunes that he managed to squeeze out were about sadness and loss. He thought about his son, he ate, he slept, but he did little else. The weather had changed too. The mornings would start with that mist that the summer sun would promise to burn off, but it never did. The days remained foggy, damp and cold. When he looked to see where his son had gone, he could see as far as the brook but no further. He felt that if he strayed far from his cottage he would get lost in his own land.

People came to visit from time to time, bringing him food and taking his sad songs to pass on to the world. But they brought no news of his son. Only of a world that seemed increasingly chaotic — of lawless governments, of rampant disease, of new hallucinogenic drugs that could make people see terrible and strange things. The world, it seemed, was speeding up and was crying out for help. His tunes were well received but they only reflected the state of things and didn't lift the spirits.

And all the time he thought of his son being out there in that increasingly dangerous world and he could do nothing to protect him.

It was then, in his deepest melancholy, that he realised that it was *peace* that was needed. His sad tunes may have reflected the mood of the world but it was *peace* that the world needed. Time to reflect, draw from nature, take strength from all the goodness that was around. He stopped hanging his head and lifted his face up to the skies. He breathed and was present in his body, finding that it was no longer an inconvenient ageing obstacle but a vessel for thought and feeling. No longer did he seek speed but instead the measuredness of old age and the patience of a life lived with love.

And so came his time of slow music. It brought him peace and made his small domain a place of peacefulness. People came, not for the music but for the peace that his cottage and garden gave them in their shattered world. Mystics came, old widows came, young couples, politicians, nurses, taxmen, and even dogs. Yes, dogs could come and rest — away from their territories there was no need for them to bark or growl. Less came in the winter when the brook froze over. Maybe a wise man, maybe a lost girl. But they came and he played them his peace.

VI

Two winters came and went and the old Melody Weaver was beginning to accept that he may never see his son again. Then one spring morning, a strange thing happened: a young man appeared with a drum made of skin and sat down on the other side of the brook and started to play and sing. The music was nothing like the Melody Weaver had ever heard. A subtle rhythm on the drum accompanied a song in a language that he didn't recognise. He guessed that it was from the far south and he got the gist of its yearning for love. But to hear singing and drums was new to the Melody Weaver. New too, was the idea that someone should bring *him* music. His craft had always been handed down through generations and the music of the Melody Weavers had been handed out to the world. But never the other way round! He didn't know whether to be angry that such a young man should have the nerve to bring him music rather than coming to receive it.

The singing and drumming went on for some time. People came and sat by the young man and listened. The Weaver went in and made tea for all of them and thought about his feelings of resentment and how he should behave towards this stranger.

When he came out with small cups and bowls for the assembled company, the young musician was singing in a language that the Weaver understood:

'What of the future, what of the past?
Yes, I care, Yes, I care.
What of the future, what of the past?
In the air, in the air.
Listen to my song.'

The refrain was picked up by the people around and the Weaver found he was singing it himself. Finally overcoming his feeling of self importance, he crossed over the brook and sat down by the young singer and handed him a small bowl of tea. The singer stopped and took the bowl, bowing his head and saying, 'thank you, master.'

'Thank you,' replied the Weaver. 'Your music is very strange to me — I have never heard anything like it. Where are you from?'

'Thank you,' said the young man, not replying directly to his question. 'I hope you like it. It is my own...'

'You own that music? You created it yourself?' The Weaver was surprised. He had assumed that there must be another Music Weaver far away in the south. That maybe this was someone new that he'd never heard of.

'I could say that, yes, I created it, but all music comes from somewhere... hidden. And... there is a man in the south who is teaching us how to find it. There are many, now, who can create their own melodies and write their own songs, but it all comes from somewhere... and... I thought you might be able to tell me... er... where.'

The Melody Weaver was staggered. A teacher who was able to show people how to find music in that hidden place, the heart. And this young man had clearly found something unique to himself.

'Why me?' he asked, after he had been silent to settle his breathing. 'You have come a long way to ask me...'

'The man who taught me, told me to ask you. He said that you had shown him...'

'My son,' the Melody Weaver burst out, his heart racing. 'You've seen my son?'

'I can't tell you...'

'Can you at least tell me his name?'

'He is called the Melody Teacher. That is all I know.'

'And how does he look, the Melody Teacher?'

'He is very pale and his hair is almost white. No, he cannot be your son — he looks so different from you. He looks so frail.'

The Melody Weaver thought to himself that this teacher must be his son, though he didn't want to believe it — so frail. He didn't want his son to be frail. At that moment, he didn't want to know any more.

Scattered Chapters   87

'So what can I tell you?' he asked the young man.

'Where does music come from?

The Melody Weaver took deep breath and said, quietly:

'It comes from here' — he pointed to the young man's navel.

'It comes from here' — he pointed to his heart.

'It comes from here' — he pointed to his forehead.

'It comes from here' — he pointed to each hand in turn.

'It comes from here' — he pointed to the ground in front of him.

'It comes from here' — he pointed up to the sky.

'And here it is, all the time' — he pointed to the brook that ran in front of his cottage. 'It's like this, like a river that is there all the time, forever flowing.'

The young man looked into the Melody Weaver's eyes, nodded, stood up and left without saying a word. The Weaver and his guests looked at the young musician as he strode off down the path to the south, his skin drum on his back.

VII

Weeks passed and no news came back to the Melody Weaver about his son. He returned to his peaceful existence and, once again, people came to share his peace and his wisdom. He made his slow music and created an oasis of calm in a world that was becoming increasingly fractious.

Then, little by little, news came to him of other musicians like the young man with the drum. There seemed to be more and more of them coming up from the south. He heard tales of songs of love, songs of protest, songs of wealth, songs of starvation; musicians forming groups. Like a benevolent virus, the music of many people seemed to be spreading through the known world.

But none came to see him again, and he didn't leave his cottage by the forests of the north to find them. So his music got slower and slower until one day he stopped. He sat out in front of his home and looked into the early morning mist in wonder and sadness. Had he lost everything? Had he found what his soul really searched for? Did he need to weave his beautiful melodies, or had the world now gone a different way? Was it time for him to depart and join his beloved Elena as a spirit in the woods and mountains of the north?

He looked and looked out over the brook and as he did so, he saw a dark figure coming towards him through the thinning mist. The figure was carrying something and as it got clearer, he could see that it was a woman carrying a child. A gentle breeze came and pushed away the last thin strands of vapour and the sun shone full on the woman's face. Her skin was the colour of ebony and her head was shaved. The Melody Weaver gasped for he had never seen anyone with such a dark skin, and then he gasped again when he saw the child that she carried. Her skin was dark like her mother's but her hair was so fair that it was almost white. The child was sleeping but the mother's eyes gleamed white in the bright morning sun. Then, as she came closer, he saw a tear roll down her cheek, then another, and he saw that her mouth, which he had thought was smiling, was actually in a frown of sadness.

She stepped over the brook and he stood up to greet her.

'What is it, my child?' he said.

'This,' she replied, holding her child out to him, 'is your granddaughter.'

'No,' he said, and stepped away from her. He turned and went back into his cottage, closing the door.

'How can this be my granddaughter?' he said to himself. 'Her skin is a completely different colour. She comes from some strange place in the south — she could be anyone. First I get a young man who claims he has been told to come to me by what I suspect is my son. Now I get a completely foreign woman claiming family allegiance. If that is my son's daughter, why isn't he with them? Why doesn't he come back to me and explain what he has done?' Then he put his head in his hands and wept, for in his heart of hearts he knew why his son had not returned.

Outside the cottage, the woman sat down and nursed her child who had just woken up with a plaintive cry. She looked at the brook and the last of the mist clearing to reveal the rolling hills and woodland that she had just struggled through. She was so tired. She had come such a long way and she had nowhere to go. In her head she heard the mantra that she had been taught:

'*North must meet south,*
East must meet west.'

And she started to intone it as she rocked her baby back to sleep.

'*North must meet south,*
East must meet west.'

The door of the cottage opened behind her and the Melody Weaver stood on the threshold, holding a tray with with oatcakes, cheese and tea on it.

'*North must meet south,*
East must meet west.'

The Melody Weaver knelt down beside her and laid the tray down in front of her.

'Where did you hear that?' he asked in astonishment.

'From Yasha, your son,' she replied.

'Yasha? So you've been with him? How is he? Why isn't he here?'

At this point the child woke up again and instinctively reached out to the Melody Weaver. He saw her eyes, then. They were Elena's eyes and he realised that her extraordinary hair was like Elena's.

'She really is my granddaughter?' he asked. 'She is, isn't she?'

'Yes, her name's Eshe.' So saying she handed her child to the Melody Weaver and he smiled a sad smile as he looked down into her eyes,

'Eshe,' he murmured. 'What a lovely name.'

'It means 'life',' the woman said.

'Life.' The Melody Weaver marvelled at the small creature that he held

in his arms. So perfect — so strange — such a mixture of south and north.

He looked at the woman who must be so tired from her travels. Indeed, she was drooping from exhaustion with hardly the energy to pick up and eat the food that he had placed in front of her. It was as though, with the Melody Weaver's acceptance of his granddaughter, all the energy that had kept her going through her arduous journey had left her.

'Come my daughter,' he said, kindly. 'You must eat and rest and then we can talk.'

VIII

When the woman had rested and fed and restored her energy, she sat down with The Melody Weaver, her child asleep on her lap, and told her story as they sat by the brook, warmed by the afternoon sun.

'My name is Binta and I come from the deep south where the great river flows and the endless forest frames the world. My father is the Rhythm Maker and his drumming is famed throughout the south. Many have come to see us to learn the drumming skills and take away my father's rhythm patterns. We live close to the endless forest in a house built of living trees. It has been there for centuries and grows and shrinks as parts die and new growth springs from the earth.

As I said, many people have come to learn but though they take away my father's creations they never create anything of their own. Or at least they didn't before your son, Yasha came.

We were startled when he first appeared. We didn't know what to make of him. He was so pale, we thought he must be ill. He spoke a language that we didn't understand and made music that we had never heard before. After a while he learnt some of our language and we learnt some of his.

As for his music, it didn't make any sense to start with. So upside down — so little rhythm, so much other sound. We learnt that this was melody and that he was bringing us this new music to share and that it was from you, the Melody Weaver of the north. He told us that his mother, who had passed into the northern forests, had given this mantra to him:

'North must meet south,
East must meet west.'

This was strange and surprised us because my mother had passed into the endless forest and told us the same thing the other way round:

'South must meet north,
West must meet east.'

In my faith, our faith, we have great belief in prophesies and this seemed like one that we were meant to take notice of. So we asked your son to stay and live with us until we had worked out what this meant.

Scattered Chapters   91

At that time, there was much unrest and disease in the cities of the north. So many young people had disappeared from the countryside around us to find their fortunes in the cities. But now stories were coming down to us that there was fighting and starvation and a terrible disease that was spreading everywhere. We hoped we were safe there. We are not skilled in fighting, only in music. As for the disease, we did our best to keep isolated from people that came down from the north. We built an encampment on the other side of the great river, where people who wanted to learn could stay for a while to make sure that they were not ill.

Yasha and my father spent a lot of time together at this time, comparing notes, exchanging ideas, learning from each other, in fact. And at the centre of this was the question in our minds about my mother's and Yasha's mother's prophecy.

At the same time, things became complicated between me and Yasha. We fell in love and felt such a love for each other that can hardly be described in music, let alone words. My father did not approve at first. We were a different colour, a different race, and people might reject us and our children or exclude them from their society. Besides, it was distracting Yasha from the very important task of understanding the meaning of our mothers' words.

Then a terrible thing happened. Some people who had come from the north to learn from my father and had stayed a while over the river in the encampment to make sure that they were not ill, came and sat with Yasha and my father to learn from them. After they had left, one by one we all fell ill. Some of us just had mild coughs but others found that they couldn't breathe. Yasha became seriously ill and, because I had recovered so quickly, I was able to care for him. It took weeks and at one point I thought that he would die. But he recovered and, because we had been so close and I had shown my dedication and love for him, my father, who had also recovered after a long fight, saw things in a different light and we were able to marry.

But something had changed in my Yasha. He became more thoughtful, quieter. He spent much time in contemplation. Sometimes we would sit together for hours just watching the wind make patterns on the great river. I wondered if he would ever fully recover — he seemed so frail, so quiet.

Then, one day, he started to teach. He taught the kitchen staff, he taught the gardener, he taught the plumber and the builder. And he showed them how to look inside and find their own music — to come into contact with the ever-flowing stream of consciousness just under the surface of their minds. The results were surprising: tunes and songs and rhythms came from his pupils that were rough hewn and simple but were authentic, not copies of music given by the masters.

To start with, my father was worried. He saw this new wave of creativity as anarchic and potentially damaging to the course and progress of music.

'Teach them your tunes, my patterns, they are better, stronger,' he said.

But Yasha replied: 'Doesn't every soul have its own music? Shouldn't everyone who wants to, be able to find their own music within themselves? They can learn and play our music and find huge value in that, but isn't the greater thing to spread the spirit of music so that all can find their own?'

'I don't know what you mean, but I shall see what happens and put a stop to it if it doesn't work,' my father said.

But it was too late. People had heard of this new thing — of learning to find their own tunes and songs and rhythms. They came to learn at Yasha's feet and many went away with a new confidence and spread the word. There were some who found it too hard and preferred to learn Yasha's and my father's music but that was all right too. 'Perhaps they have some other fountain within them,' Yasha used to say.

It was around this time that I found myself with child. I would sing to the unborn mystery inside me, songs that I never knew existed. They were for her, they came from her.

People kept on coming to learn and we were increasingly worried that the disease that was so threatening would come back, brought by an unsuspecting pupil and kill us all. It was a hard time with so many wanting to learn. Yasha would go across to the encampment in a boat and teach them from a distance. Sometimes groups of musicians would come and show him what had happened — how the music had expanded. Love songs, protest songs, songs of worship, of war, of nature, would filter across the river to us, and my father was moved.

'This is new,' he said. 'All is changing. The world has expanded and is in trouble, but it needs its music — it needs to make it every day in every place. See what we get back now? Sounds I had never thought of — every soul lit up by its own music.'

But all this teaching took its toll on Yasha. My beautiful frail husband became frailer still while the music of the world expanded around us.

'See what has happened?' he said to me one night. 'The power which was invested in a few of us has now spread so far that it cannot be stopped. My work is almost done.'

I felt relief then. To think that he could rest now and fully recover. I was close to my time — the child inside me was urging to come out into the world. The night she came, my Eshe, Yasha was still across the river teaching. When he heard, he rushed back and came to me and held our child in his arms.

There were tears in his eyes as he said to me: 'My time is not long now. I have done all I can and my work is finished. Soon, I must go and join the spirit of my mother.'

'No!' I cried. 'Don't leave us. We need you!'

'I know,' he replied. 'But our love is so strong that I will be with you always. It will cross continents; it will cross the world.' He embraced me then and I could feel him shaking with fatigue.

'Go and rest now,' I said. 'You'll feel better in the morning and then we can talk.'

'I will stay here with you,' he said. 'And sleep here on the floor beside you.'

And he lay down and went to sleep.

Detail

My new child woke a few times in the night and I fed her straight away so as not to disturb Yasha. On one occasion I could hear him murmuring in his sleep:

'North must meet south,
East must meet west.'
'North must meet south,
East must meet west.'

Then there was a pause and he said quite clearly:

'Binta, you must take Eshe to my father in the north. She will be the next Melody Weaver.'

But when I asked him what he meant, he was sound asleep and I couldn't rouse him.

I awoke the next morning to find that he had gone. Shakily and with a lot of effort, I got out of bed and took Eshe with me to try and find him. It was early still and no one else was awake. I called his name gently but got no reply. Some instinct made me walk out towards the endless forest that encircles the world, and there, caught in the early rays of the sun, I could see him walking towards the forest. As he walked he seemed to become transparent and wispy until I could just make out his outline before he disappeared completely.

Then I knew that he had gone to join his mother — he had told me how she had faded and disappeared into the great forest of the north and now he had done just the same.

I called his name but all that came back was the echo of my voice from the forest wall.

IX

When Binta had finished her tale, she lay down exhausted on the mat she had been sitting on and went to sleep. The Melody Weaver took the baby Eshe from her and cradled her in his arms.

'So you are the new Melody Weaver to be,' he said gently, looking down into her grey, sparkling eyes, her ebony face, her silver hair. 'You are *'North meets South'*. Are you the dawn of a new time? A time when music is made everywhere? What has your father unleashed in you, in the world? Should I call you Aurora?'

He couldn't take his eyes off her. He just held her as she looked up at him with her father's eyes, her grandmother's eyes, the eyes of the north in the face of the south. What did this all mean?

After a while, Eshe became hungry again and cried for her mother's milk. The Melody Weaver gently woke Binta and turned his back and went into the cottage as she suckled her child. He returned with a tray laden with good food — food from the forest, food from the lands that surrounded his small domain. They ate together in silence, the babbling brook for company, and when she had eaten her fill, Binta smiled at her father-in-law and said:

'This food is beautiful but simple. I can enrich it for you, if you like, with herbs and spices as is the custom in the south.'

The Melody Weaver looked at her then and smiled and said, 'Just a little, for I am an old man now and used to simple food.' Then he smiled even more broadly and put out his hand. 'So you will stay then? With your new child? And help me look after her? And you shall learn of my skills and I shall learn of yours? And Eshe Aurora shall learn from us both?'

'I will,' she said. 'But what is this new name you have given her? Aurora?'

'Aurora means dawn, and you told me that Eshe means life. She is the dawn of a new life. A life of music. A life that my son has bequeathed to us.'

They both cried, then, for the loss of Yasha — she who had seen him fade and he who hoped above all to see him again.

At least now, the Melody Weaver knew that his son had been loved and that every time he looked down into his granddaughter's eyes he would see his son there too, looking out, looking far.

And Binta? What of her? She knew, with a deep knowledge, that she could keep all that had happened in her heart and that her Yasha would always be there too.

So this is what happened — the rhythm of the south met the melody of the north and produced a new dawn of music. The spell that the Melody Weaver's son had broken meant that all could now share in this dawn, this Aurora of music. And the known world became whole for the first time.

Detail

Scattered Chapters

Ann Pollard **Heartsong**
Oil on Canvas
150 cm by 100 cm

Heartsong

Optimism. Have you ever thought how hard that is? Look at any good story with an optimistic end and it has to start with a struggle — with something going wrong. A story that starts with everything being hunky-dory and potters along merrily to the end is not an optimistic one. There's no hoping for better times or getting to a better place because you're there already, and people don't write those sort of stories unless they're trying to sell you something like holidays or Timeshares or pensions or shoes or whatever you might feel you'd like to make your life better. Whoops! I caught myself out, there! That part of that story is optimistic! You're hoping to make your life better!

So, happy — happy stories are boring. We don't want to hear them. We'd rather listen to the NEWS: start the day with the worst things: floods, pandemics, despotic presidents, incompetent governments, sex scandals or worse. Things can only get better after breakfast. Is this optimism? Well, it's not a very optimistic start — optimism is not inherently sown into these NEWS stories, except for a few. Try working out how many of these NEWS stories promise a better tomorrow or are about people doing good things to, or for, other people, or new discoveries that could save the world. There are a few but quite clearly people who write the NEWS stories think, or perhaps they know, that we would rather be told about the worst things that are happening. Maybe they're right — forewarned is forearmed!

So where are we heading here? We start with a day filled with other people's catastrophes, other people's problems, and that makes us feel better, does it? Have you ever had that feeling of relief when you hear really bad news? 'Oh well, that's it we're buggered! We might as well give up! There's nothing we can do about it! It's up to someone else now!'

Relief! But that isn't optimism. It's Sod's law, Murphy's law, if anything can go wrong it will! Perhaps sometimes it's relief that it didn't happen to us. This moody start to the day doesn't have optimism sown into it. It's the opposite — it's pessimistic.

Optimism to my mind, needs to have the seeds of improvement sown into it. In fact, come to think of it, seeds are intrinsically optimistic: plant them in the ground, wait for sun and rain and up they pop! But hang on a moment, in my book, gardening is hard work. Seeds don't just pop up because you planted them, they need looking after. You have to turn the earth to make it moist and receptive — hard work. You have to nourish your seeds with compost (hopefully your own, with NO PEAT involved) — more hard work. You have to protect them from frost, torrential rain, careless feet and footballs. So there is something in the seed idea that really points to optimism.

It's the same with music. You start with a seed of an idea. It may have got planted in your unconscious some time ago or it may be brand new, but it's a seed and you have to work with it and the main driving force

Scattered Chapters   97

is... optimism. But like I said, the seed needs work to grow. Now, if you're a musician, a lot of the work has been done. You've learnt to play your instrument. You've actually fallen in love with it — it has grabbed your heart. You've worked to find your own sound. You will probably have your own unique way of playing. You have listened to others and learnt from them. And all this has taken a long time.

But now you have a new seed and it can be nerve-wracking: the seed sounds so good, will I wreck it? Is it truly mine or did I inadvertently nick it from someone else? You need optimism! You need to take the plunge and follow this seed, this phrase, this tune, wherever it goes. That takes guts, and if you read any fables or fairy stories that turn out well, the main character has guts.

So you've prepared your ground, turned your earth, and now all that you've learnt or didn't even know you'd learnt comes to fruition. But then you must do two things — capture it, and give it freedom...

It strikes me that music is inherently optimistic — perhaps the most optimistic thing that humans create. Music without words, that is. Words can screw things up terribly as most bluegrass songs show. But music gives people hope. It's what they turn to when they need solace, reassurance that things will turn out okay, a way to rise from their depression. The seed of music is sown, the struggle begins, the questions are asked: and then we have the answer. It's all there, but there are no words to worry about, just a mystery of a musical answer.

And here's a strange thing: often the saddest music is the most optimistic — Barber's Adagio for instance, or slower music by Beethoven, Mozart, or Schubert, or romantics like Mahler and Brahms. They come to you in your depths of darkness and lead you out into the light. I have been written to by many Harry Potter fans about my 'Dumbledore's Farewell' — the saddest piece I ever wrote — and they have told me how it rescued them, led them out of depression, gave them hope.

But there is another kind of optimistic music. Uplifting, joyful, and very difficult to get right. Overdo it and it sounds banal, shallow, manipulative. But get it right and you have 'Heartsong' — a song from the heart, a song *of* the heart. Here is a piece of music that stands out from most of the music written for guitar. It's big, it's loud, it's powerful, it can fill a vast hall with its joyful resonance. It is optimism made sound, it is...

Enough said.

Listen.

Artist Profiles

Ann Pollard

Ann's painting is driven by the medium and a lifelong love of working with paint. Her aim is to achieve spontaneous and exciting effects which have something in common with nature. The "accidental" approach to technique and interpretation is borne of confidence, experimentation, and an Oriental approach to the subject. Her work seems familiar and Impressionist in style but there is nothing traditional about her working method. There is an energy and simplicity in the compositions but the texture tells another story. A lightness of touch that can impart a detail that seems at odds with the heavily applied paint. Ann works mainly in oils to produce a range of contemporary visual experiences with a sense of peace. A quiet and personal reflection of the landscape but with an energetic undertone and a bold palette.

Ann has worked as a professional Artist for the past 20 years. Teaching, Painting and Crafts, in Derbyshire. Ann opened her own Studio in Derbyshire where she taught painting techniques between 2004 and 2012. She has held multiple successful exhibitions selling her work internationally. More recently she has moved to Nottinghamshire and her work may be found in Independent Galleries throughout the UK.

Jan Gay

Jan creates a very personal response to her surroundings, whether landscape, figure or still life. She has always felt that observation underpins everything that she creates, but over the years she has wanted to develop something more from a subject.

"Art is not a predictable journey. I aim to sift out the essentials of an image without actually losing the subject. This can be a challenge – there often seems to be an argument between detail and simplicity, but it's worth the struggle!"

Her desire to look beyond the superficial, simplifying shape and exploring abstract elements brings a quality to her work which goes beyond realism.

Teaching art has been another aspect of Jan's career. She has enjoyed sharing her passion for painting, working with adults in the community and people with health issues, demonstrating the need for creativity in life. She obtained a B.A. in Birmingham in the early 1990s, specialising in painting, with some ceramics and printmaking. Prior to that time, she studied painting and ceramics when she completed her B Ed in Sussex. Jan has exhibited in London and galleries throughout the UK and she became a member of the Royal Birmingham Society of Artists in 2008. She has enjoyed the privilege of living in different parts of the country, and is currently based in Solihull in the West Midlands.

Jan Gay RBSA
www.jangay.co.uk
Instagram: jangayart
www.etsy.com/uk/shop/jangayart/

Trudy Good

Although Good did begin an academic art education she opted out after a year, disillusioned with the institution and wanting to find her own path uninfluenced by current trends and teachings. In an effort to discover her own artistic preferences, she began over a decade long journey of continued self- instruction and independent study. After a 15-year love affair with the immediacy of drawing, Good's creative journey took a sudden unplanned fork in her journey when she began working in oils. Although the medium was relatively new, her aesthetic remains the same, to create something that is beautiful and well crafted.

The popularity of Good's work has continued to grow globally, with successful exhibitions in many cities including, London, New York, Miami, Los Angeles, Hong Kong and Sydney as well as Europe. She has also been lucky enough to collaborate with many top couture designers and has worked on specific projects for London Fashion week.

Danny O'Connor

Danny O'Connor is from Liverpool and was born 2nd August 1981. He studied Graphic Arts at Liverpool John Moores Art School.

His work is a celebration of contrasts focusing mainly on portraits and figures with a prevalence of opposing artistic influences. Danny's inspiration walks a tightrope between high and lowbrow sources as diverse as comics, illustration, character design, digital art and graffiti to Abstract Expressionism, Cubism, German Expressionism, Futurism, Art Nouveau, Baroque, Rococo and beyond all — pulled together to create hyper stylised and abstracted works. Contrasts play a big role in what he does — it's probably the most resounding feature throughout all of Danny's work in one way or another. He likes to mix natural flowing lines with harsh diagonals.

Clean crisp areas of colour with layered messy splashes of paint — trying to achieve something that appears both modern and almost futuristic whilst retaining a raw traditional aesthetic. The paintings are built up in layer upon layer of paint which give the pieces great depth of field. They are created with an arsenal of tools that don't settle with convention. As well as the more widely acknowledged paint and brush Danny uses all manner of mediums such as correction fluid, spray paint, ink, paint markers, texture pastes, charcoal, graphite and collage. All applied in an equally diverse manner using brushes, fingers, paint rollers, sticks, paper and cardboard to drip, splash, spray, print and stroke the paint onto the surface.

Danny's work has been exhibited worldwide including London, New York, Los Angeles, Barcelona, Amsterdam, Jakarta and Hong Kong. Commercial collaborations include book artwork for New York Times Best-selling authors Colleen Hoover and Tarryn Fisher. Artwork for the TV show *Confess* and clothing collaboration with international fashion brand Ellesse.

Rachel Tighe

Rachel has been a self-employed artist for the past nine years after building up a reputation with galleries and clients since graduating from university in 2008. Her work has been exhibited in solo shows, and recognisable art fairs from London to New York. Rachel describes her work as "bold, colourful and naïve in nature; it represents how I see my surroundings in an expressive and fluid form. I think that over the years my style has become more refined and my use of colour has directed me into exploring new thoughts and compositions. I feel that by exploring ideas alone in my studio has steered me to develop naturally and hone in on my style."

To sum up her practice Rachel says it's about the exploration of mark making and instinctive lines that map out and form our conscious surroundings. The graphical nature of her strokes challenges her use of colour to create depth and balance. Rachel loves landscapes and florals to draw inspiration from as there are so many compositions and shapes from architecture that seem complex, but when painting it becomes so effortless and free-flowing. She looks for certain outlines and characteristics when creating a painting.

Website: www.racheltighe.com
Instagram: @racheltighe
Twitter: @Rachel_Tighe

Roy Meats

Roy was born in Nottingham, the son of a lace maker and a lorry driver. His love for art and drawing was always evident and he started to sell his paintings whilst still at school. As his art progressed. he found inspiration for nearly all his paintings came from his love of music. Either a line in a song, or the title would give Roy the idea and he could then tell that story in his paintings.

Roy says, "I have found that "everyone" has that one song that conjures up a memory for them.

http://www.roymeatsart.co.uk/
https://www.facebook.com/roy.meats

Carl Knibb

Carl Knibb is a Staffordshire based artist, who works from his studio in the city of Lichfield. His work is dedicated to capturing light — from the changing light of natural landscapes, to the sparkle of water, the shadows and reflections of a street scene, and the play of light on a figure. He is intrigued by what light can both hide and highlight. In 2018, Carl was chosen to compete in Sky Arts Landscape Artist of the Year. He won his heat with his painting of Fountains Abbey. In 2017, Carl's painting of Lichfield Cathedral won first place in the Lichfield Cathedral 'Capture the Cathedral' competition. As part of this award his painting was exhibited alongside works by J M W Turner. Over the last two years, Carl has contributed several articles to The Artist magazine, and his work has appeared in magazines published as far afield as South Africa.

Carl is often drawn to scenes that have some kind of interaction within them, whether that's the flow and pattern of people in the street, or the relationship of light and shadow within a landscape. He works in acrylics and oils, often sketching en plein air to try to capture a fleeting moment, then returning to his studio to expand on that idea. Carl's paintings can take anything from a few hours to complete, to many weeks. Carl can be contacted via his website carlknibb.com, and through Facebook (Carl Knibb, artist), and Instagram (Carl Knibb, artist). He can also be emailed direct via lionhouseart@gmail.com

Blandine Anderson

Blandine trained in Ceramics as a Fine Art — and after five years of lecturing in colleges in the South West of England, established her first professional studio in Devon in 1989, producing unique pieces, individually hand-built in porcelain and stoneware.

Her subjects are creatures in landscape and nature is her passion but Blandine's ideas are steered and designs dominated by composition and proportion.

She uses creatures to "populate" and enhance base-forms: some creatures such as hares and foxes create long fluid lines, while others such as sheep, punctuate or add a "musical" rhythm to the composition.

Depending on the size of the addition, the scale and perspective of the piece can be completely transformed.

Some of Blandine's works feature additional themes such as: folklore, cartography, music, poetry, natural history, chemistry, quantum physics and astronomy. Her work is not moulded or repeated, each piece is a "one off". Coloured porcelain slips are applied at the greenware stage, which are stencilled, painted, stamped and incised. After glazing, the work is fired to Stoneware at 1245 Centigrade.

Website: www.blandineanderson.com

Sonja Burliston

Sonja is a printmaker and illustrator based in Bristol. Her work is warm and vibrant, often centring around people and their connections with each other. She enjoys a balance of printing personal work, running print workshops and Illustrating for clients. Since discovering silk screen printing, it has been her primary medium. Her prints are made from separate layers of colour applied through hand painted or drawn stencils.

"Words, and the stories and poems they form, give me direction and inspiration in my life and visual work. Responding to Nick Hooper's writing for this project got the sap rising and ideas flowing. I decided to high-light the theme 'Welcome' because new life and new beginnings can be scary but are beautiful and that word is a reminder to greet that cycle of change with open arms. Welcome, fresh and delicate crocus!"
Her Instagram is @sonja.burnie
Her online shop is https://sonjaburnie.bigcartel.com/

Chloe Doyle

Chloe is a Derby born artist who has been drawing and painting since childhood. Chloe attended the Round House College acquiring three art diplomas and an award in drawing from the London College of Art and later a brief spell at De Montfort University.

Sue Martin

Although specialising in portraiture, Sue Martin has illustrated books and produced artwork for CD covers and advertising. She is best known for her detailed coloured pencil drawings but also enjoys working in oils and watercolours. Some of Sue's paintings and drawings have been published as limited edition prints that have sold internationally.

Sue takes inspiration from her passions. Sue's love of music inspired her to produce a print series of 9 paintings entitled 'Music Studies' – based on musical instruments; the first 6 (each with a run of 850) sold out within 18 months and over the past few years Sue has been building a portrait portfolio of musicians which she plans to exhibit next year. Sue lives within the South Downs National Park and her recent paintings and prints have evolved from the beauty of the countryside and her wildlife photography.

Website: www.suemartinportraits.com
Facebook: www.facebook.com/suemartinportraits
Instagram: www.instagram.com/suemartinart

Emma Wood

Emma Wood is an artist and designer who specialises in making high-quality, desirable, fused-glass artworks. Her work is a constantly evolving range of original, distinctive designs.

After taking time to raise a family, Emma has worked for several independents and now has taken the opportunity to run her own glass art company.

Each individual piece is hand-made by Emma, using ranges of colour, texture and the light-specific qualities of glass to produce fused panels of striking beauty and detail.

Gary O'Neil

British artist Gary O'Neil was born in Birmingham, England. The desire to draw, paint, make marks, and create pictures was apparent from a very early age. Influences were numerous and varied but images streaming on TV from the USA were particularly captivating, JFK, MLK, skyscrapers, mustangs, corvettes, the space race, and tall palm trees in the Californian sunshine; all were beguiling at that time.

He would later travel throughout the USA and work alongside other artists for a number of years. Returning to the UK, he pioneered airbrushing, creating graffiti-style T-shirts for tourists in a number of English coastal resorts. Completing a BA Fine Art degree, he achieved First-Class honours and was given the Ben Hartley award at Plymouth University in 2011. He has now returned to his native Birmingham where he continues to make work using various strategies to investigate the language of painting.

Val Pitchford

Val Pitchford worked in aspects of design for a number of years. Her ultimate aim was to become a full time painter. This was finally achieved over 15 years ago. She had the privilege of studying for a considerable amount of time with the gifted and immensely knowledgeable Robin Child at his Lydgate Art Research Centre. The lectures and practical experience gained were exceptional.

Val now paints full time in her Malvern Studio.

Oil is a favourite medium, generally on canvas and at times on paper. She aims to present an idea with an immediate and fresh approach. Always exploring, moving from abstract to the representational and aware of how much there is to learn especially from those who pushed the boundaries ahead.

Val has exhibited on many occasions in private galleries, in Cork Street, the Mall Galleries and as a Discerning Eye prize winner in the Triforium of the Temple Church in London.

Three of her paintings were commissioned and presented at the centenary celebrations in Fátimain Portugal, May 2017.

Val's work is in collections in the UK, on the Continent as well as in America.

About the Author

Nick Hooper (known as Nicholas Hooper in the film world) has written the music for over 200 films and has won two BAFTAs and an Ivor Novello award. He composed the soundtrack for two of the Harry Potter films, gaining a Grammy nomination for *Harry Potter and the Half Blood Prince*. Inspired by working so closely with J K Rowling's stories, he turned to writing words as well as music. Nick published his first novel *Above the Void* in 2017 and he has also published a children's book, *Bird Being*, which is illustrated by local artists in his region of West Oxfordshire.

Nick is also a guitarist of note, and has collaborated closely with Gordon Giltrap during the past decade, performing with him in concert. During Lockdown Nick created this collection of stories inspired by Gordon's and Paul Ward's latest CD, *Scattered Chapters*.

He is currently working on his trilogy 'The Art Detective' which features the loveable and intriguing Detective Inspector Arnold.

Acknowledgements

First and foremost, I want to thank Gordon Giltrap for asking me to write *Scattered Chapters* and Paul Ward for so ably and generously supporting this idea. Thanks also to Wymer Publishing for publishing my stories and putting their time and resources into the whole wonderful undertaking. Also thanks to Val for proofreading and my wife Judith for her observations in the opening two chapters.

In writing these stories I would like to acknowledge the influence of my friend Georgie Steele, an experienced and brilliant story-teller, particularly in 'The Melody Weaver's Son', which was also influenced by someone I never knew – Hermann Hesse who wrote Siddhartha. Other influences are Richard Curtis, with whom I worked on the film *The Girl in the Café* – his wistful, romantic and humorous story-telling inspired 'The Kissing Gate' and 'The Stars look down on Linda'; Charles Dickens for his *Christmas Carol*; Douglas Adams for *The Hitchhikers Guide to the Galaxy*; and Danah Zohar who wrote *The Quantum Self*.

Finally I would like to acknowledge my mother, Muriel Hooper, who wrote children's books, most notably *The Goose Girl*. She inspired me to read widely when I was young, and finally, after decades of composing music, I have found the instinct to write that she passed on to me.

Photography: Roger Newport
Additional photography: Luca Bailey (Heartsong)
Digital manipulation: Andy Bishop
Co-ordination: Jerry Bloom